WEIRD
AIRCRAFT

WEIRD
AIRCRAFT

Peter Henshaw

CHARTWELL
BOOKS, INC.

Published in 2009 by
CHARTWELL BOOKS, INC.
A division of BOOK SALES, INC.
114 Northfield Avenue
Edison, New Jersey 08837
USA

**Copyright © 2009 Regency
House Publishing Limited**
Niall House
24–26 Boulton Road
Stevenage, Hertfordshire
SG1 4QX, UK

For all editorial enquiries, please contact
Regency House Publishing at
www.regencyhousepublishing.com

ISBN-13: 978-0-7858-2404-6

ISBN-10: 0-7858-2404-9

Printed in China

CONTENTS

CHAPTER ONE

EXCELLENT ADVENTURES

'We are still far from the ultimate goal,' declared the U.S. War Department. It was referring to human flight, and the pronouncement was made in December 1903. But only five days later, the Wright brothers were to prove it wrong, sparking off a firestorm of aeronautical innovation that within a few years would see aircraft of a power, speed and controllability of which the Wright brothers, let alone sceptical War Department officials, could only dream.

ABOVE: Professor George Francis Fitzgerald attempts to fly at College Park, Dublin in 1895, using towed gliders.

OPPOSITE: E.P. Frost with his Ornithopter No. 2 in the early 1900s.

ABOVE: The Wright Flyer I *is seen on 14 December 1903 at Kill Devil Hills, Kitty Hawk, North Carolina.*

OPPOSITE: The German Carl Jatho's 9-hp aircraft of 1903.

But there had been good reason for its pessimism, and what may now appear as chronic shortsightedness actually had some justification in the real world of 1903. For centuries, man had been attempting to emulate the birds, but every attempt had been ultimately disappointing. Balloons and gliders allowed flight of a kind, but not the controllable powered flight that would allow a pilot to take off and land at will, not to mention stay in the air for as long as he chose or for as long as his fuel held out. The U.S. Patent Office had a policy of freely granting applications for plans for ornithopters, even though their European colleagues were rather more cautious, because they assumed that heavier-than-air flight was simply not a possibility.

As for the War Department, its own disillusionment was largely the result of the failure of Samuel Pierpoint Langley's government-funded Aerodrome, a bi-winged machine powered by a 50-hp petrol engine. The Aerodrome was launched by means of a catapult atop a houseboat, floating on the Potomac river, but when it plunged into the icy waters, 'like a handful of mortar', the War Department promptly decided that the

whole concept of powered flight had been a crazy idea that could never be made to work.

Yet despite this pessimism in official circles, a steady stream of pioneers continued to strive toward that goal, despite the odds. There were two schools of thought: that wings should flap like those of a bird – as in a so-called ornithopter – or that they should be in a fixed position. The idea of an aircraft with flapping wings may seem ludicrous

ABOVE: The first failure of the manned Aerodrome on 7 October 1903.

OPPOSITE ABOVE: The Aerodrome, after it was rebuilt and flown over Lake Keuka by Glenn Curtiss in 1914.

today, and the Italian theorist, Giovanni Borelli, had already demonstrated in the 17th century why they could not lift a human being into the air. Yet for many, the idea continued to exert a particular and compelling fascination.

It seemed logical enough, given that the inspiration for manned flight came from birds, bats and insects, that flew by flapping their wings, and throughout the 19th century many designs made it onto the drawing board, though fewer were actually built and fewer still attempted to fly. None of them actually made it into the air under its own power, with a pilot on board, although some scale models did have a modicum of success. There was an apparent breakthrough in 1809, when the Austrian, Jacob Degen, claimed to have successfully flown an ornithopter, which in a way he had, having succeeded in making giant hops across a parade ground, and later performing this feat in front of crowds in Paris and Vienna. But the craft had been tethered to a hot-air balloon, and it was this that had provided the lift rather than Degen's flapping wings.

Ornithopter adherents persisted in their determination to emulate birds in the most obvious way, well up to the time that the Wright brothers made their breakthrough flight. One such well-known experimenter was E.P. Frost, an Englishman who built several different machines over more than a decade, and who was convinced that artificial wings, using real birds' feathers, were the key to getting off the ground. In this, he had been inspired not only by the birds but also by the myth of Daedalus and his son, Icarus, who attempted to escape imprisonment by King Minos of Crete, for whom Daedalus had constructed the labyrinth, by building wings using feathers and beeswax.

Early in the 16th century, John Damian, the Abbot of Tungland in Galloway, Scotland, leapt from the walls of Stirling Castle, intending to flap his way to France. Alas, he plunged straight to earth, and was fortunate to escape with no more than a broken thighbone. Damian later blamed his crash on the fact that he had used feathers taken from the flightless dunghill fowl, rather than from an eagle, which he claimed would undoubtedly have allowed him to soar.

Of course, birds' wings are a miracle of nature, and have a high strength-to-weight ratio that provides excellent lift. E.P. Frost used thousands of feathers in the construction of his machines, fashioning wings for them out of canes and silk. He also tried steam power, using a 3-hp BAT petrol engine in his 1903 ornithopter (*page 9*), but none of his creations proved capable of lifting him off the ground.

One might have expected ornithopter enthusiasts to have bowed to the inevitable by 1911; after all, by then fixed-wing aircraft were regularly flying on both sides of the Atlantic, one setting a new distance record of around 300 miles (480km), while Louis Blériot had successfully flown across the English Channel. None of this deterred H.J.B. Passat, however, who dispensed with the feathers while persisting with a modern ornithopter, which in some respects was relatively advanced, in that it had a 4.5-hp motorcycle engine and a welded steel-tube frame.

Despite French dominance in the aeronautical field, Passat's ornithopter was tested on Wimbledon Common, England, in 1912, and did actually fly, even though the 'flight' was little more than a hop of 400ft (120m) at a speed of 15mph (24km/h). The day's activities ended when Passat hit a tree, but he persevered, going on to build improved machines over the next few years, even though it was becoming clear that the future lay in fixed-wing aircraft. Although Passat's flapping wings had performed to a limited extent, he had no way of controlling the craft, and was unable to take off, steer, climb, descend or land at will.

STEAMING AHEAD
Fixed wings, therefore, were to prove essential to achieving sufficient lift, with a relatively lightweight, powerful engine providing aerodynamic thrust via propellers. The wings presented no

problems, although the larger they were the more ungainly was the bracing required, but sourcing a suitable engine was a more difficult matter. By the mid-19th century, steam engines were powering anything from cotton mills to railway locomotives and even flying machines. In 1828, Vittorio Sarti built a primitive steam-powered helicopter, followed 14 years later by the Englishman W.H. Phillips, who, almost 50 years after Sir George Cayley's first powered models of helicopters that had been driven by elastic devices, constructed a steam-driven model helicopter that weighed 20lbs (9kg).

The problem with steam power was that the engines had a low power-to-weight ratio which, although it was no problem for a massive unit bolted to a factory floor, was more of an issue where aircraft were concerned. Sir Hiram Maxim, who also invented the machine gun, believed he had the answer and used heavy, powerful steam engines, housed in massive airframes, and wings that would hopefully generate sufficient lift to fly. To give some idea of the scale: Maxim's flying machine had 4,000sq ft (370m[2]) of wing area, much of it on a huge octagonal centre section, the total wingspan being 104ft (32m). The two 180-hp compound engines were supplied with steam from a marine boiler, which was remarkably compact and powerful. It was only 8-ft (2.4-m) long, weighed less than 1,000lbs (454kg), and used a multiplicity of copper tubes to deliver over 3,000lbs of pressure to the engines. The engines, in turn, drove two propellers, each one of them being 17ft 10in (5.4m) across.

Maxim's machine dwarfed bystanders, and was possibly the biggest flying machine of its day, having taken three years to build. Maxim was justifiably cautious, and when it was finally ready for testing at Baldwyn's Park in Kent, England, it was fitted with extra-heavy wheels to prevent it from taking off. The craft was damaged during this first gruelling test, although Maxim was sufficently encouraged to

proceed with the first test flight. Here again, he was cautious, and the aircraft was run along a specially laid railway track, with guard rails attached to prevent it from flying more than 2ft above the ground.

In July 1894, the Maxim machine was at last able to show what it could do, and after a run-up of 600ft (180m), at nearly 40mph (65km/h), actually took off, but with enough force to break one of the guard rails.

The engines were immediately shut down and the plane was crash-landed off its track, putting an end to the whole project. Maxim had spent a great deal of his considerable fortune developing and testing his steam-powered monster which, if he had only persevered, might eventually have proved viable; by 1915, however, it would have found itself comprehensively outpaced by the new breed of multi-engined petrol-powered machines that had by then been developed as bombers.

In a sense, Maxim had already been beaten to it. Four years before his big steamer was wheeled onto its track at Baldwyn's Park, the Frenchman,

Clement Ader's military Avion III, *displayed at the Musée de l'Air in Paris, France.*

Clement Ader, had succeeded in leaving the ground in his own steam-powered machine. He had been experimenting with flight for many years, and early in his career also believed that utilizing birds' feathers was the key to human flight. He actually built a goose-feathered 'bird', large enough to carry a man, and it worked, but it was tethered to the ground and required a strong headwind to rise, making it more like a kite than a true flying machine.

Ader, nevertheless, had learned enough from his feathered contraption to be convinced that curved fixed wings were the best solution, and *Éole* was built, being a steam-powered aircraft based on these principles. It resembled a bat rather than a bird, though significantly its foldable silk wings, with a frame of hollow ribs, could theoretically be twisted or warped to provide some control over lift. The Wright brothers would later take out a patent on wing-warping, as it came to be known.

On 9 October 1890, *Éole* was pushed out onto level ground at Château d'Armainvilliers, near Brie, south-west of Paris. Its 20-hp steam engine was fired up, and Ader set off,

actually leaving the ground, although the 'flight' was yet another of those big hops, this time one of 165ft (50m). But he was unable to control *Éole*, despite the twistable wings, and although Ader was arguably the first man to successfully take off from level ground in a powered machine, it was not a sustainable, controllable flight.

The military potential of aircraft for reconnaissance and bombing had been recognized, even at this early stage, and the French War Office was sufficiently impressed to commission Ader to build a larger, two-seater version, able to carry a 165-lb (75-kg) bomb load. *Avion III* was based on the same principles as *Éole*, but sadly proved unable to fly. The prototype was taken to a test track at Satory, near Versailles, in 1897, but only partially lifted off the ground.

The work of these pioneers was eventually eclipsed by the German, Otto Lilienthal, all of whose machines were admittedly gliders, but between 1891 and 1896 he was able to make over 2,000 flights, some of them exceeding 800ft (240m). Lilienthal's machines were both monoplane and biplane types, and he had already begun work on a powered version

when he was tragically killed in a crash on 10 August 1896. Instead of propellers, he had envisaged that the plane would be thrust along by flapping paddles on the wingtips, and it was to have been powered by a carbonic acid gas engine. Would it have worked? Who knows? But the next breakthrough was to be just around the corner.

THE BIG BANG

Only a few years after Maxim and Ader's experiments with steam power, and with Lilienthal's graceful gliders covering the greatest distances, the Austrian, William Kress, would create a new type of aircraft that was to be a true pointer to the future. Kress was a remarkable man, who in 1893, at the age of 57, had begun an engineering course at the Vienna polytechnic. Five years later, he began work on his flying machine, which was intended to be operable from both water and snow which, in the absence of an airfield, was bound to make it highly desirable.

Kress's machine had an advanced airframe, using wooden ribs and steel tubing mounted on aluminium floats; its real advance, however, was that it was powered by a petrol engine.

Steam power, as we have seen, was simply too heavy to be practicable in flying machines, but the new four-stroke petrol internal-combustion engine was an entirely different matter, and being far more compact than the equivalent steam unit had a far better power-to-weight ratio. The four-stroke principle had been invented by Nikolaus Otto in 1877, following which a practical engine was built by Gottleib Daimler seven years later, with Dr.

OPPOSITE: A facsimile of the Wright Flyer III.

RIGHT: Orville Wright, seen flying over Fort Meyer in the Wright Model A biplane in 1908.

Wolfert eventually fitting a 2-hp Daimler petrol engine to a balloon in 1888, which successfully flew.

But ten years later, when Kress designed the first petrol-powered aircraft, there was still no suitable engine available. Petrol engines were still in their infancy, and Kress's demand for a 40-hp motor, weighing 440lbs (200kg), could not be met. Mercedes came closest to supplying such a unit in 1901, its 30-hp engine tipping the scales at 840lbs (380kg). It was duly fitted to Kress's seaplane, which in October 1901 was being prepared for its first flight from the Tullnerbach reservoir. The heavy engine caused the plane to sit low in the water, but as Kress accelerated along its surface, the floats began to rise into the air. Unfortunately, the pilot had to shut down the engine as a stone groyne came into view. As he tried to manoeuvre the aircraft around it, the

wind caught the undersides of the wings, flipping the unstable machine over and causing it to break up. Kress was saved, and his machine was partially repaired, but he made no attempt to fly it again.

Although William Kress had been unsuccessful with his seaplane, his pioneering work demonstrated that, as far as powered flight was concerned,

petrol engines were the way to go. Several pioneers were able to make petrol-powered hops over the next few years, and Samuel Langley's unmanned quarter-scale model was the first to make a sustained flight using petrol power, even though his piloted Aerodrome had been less successful, causing disillusionment with the whole concept. But the greatest success was

ABOVE: In 14-bis, the Brazilian, Alberto Santos-Dumont, achieved the first flight in Europe on 12 November 1906.

OPPOSITE: The Aerial Experiment Association's Cygnet II at Baddeck Bay, Nova Scotia.

yet to come, and two unassuming bicycle salesmen from Dayton, Ohio, would be the ones to achieve it.

Orville and Wilbur Wright may not have been the first to make a powered flight, to use a petrol engine, to build a plane with fixed wings, or to make a sustained flight, but they were responsible for making a controlled flight, that was also piloted and powered, a reality, and which would make modern aircraft possible.

Some aircraft pioneers had been working on their obsession for decades, but the Wrights did not become

interested in flight until 1896, although their painstaking approach to the subject would ultimately deliver success. They collected every possible piece of information on the subject, even to the extent of entering into correspondence with established pioneers such as Samuel Langley. They built a wind tunnel behind their bicycle shop to test different wing sections, discovering in the process that most of the published data regarding aerofoils had been incorrect. The Wrights tested 200 different wing shapes, and learned much about pilot-controlled flight in the

process, while tests using full-sized gliders were to teach them a great deal more.

It was this painstaking work that enabled the Wrights to make the world's first controlled powered flight in December 1903, and less than two years later Wilbur was able to fly the improved *Flyer III* an astonishing 24 miles (39km) in a flight lasting 38 minutes. This was truly astonishing, and indicated how ahead of the field the Wrights really were, and it wasn't until November 1906 that someone else would manage a sustained flight. Although it achieved a

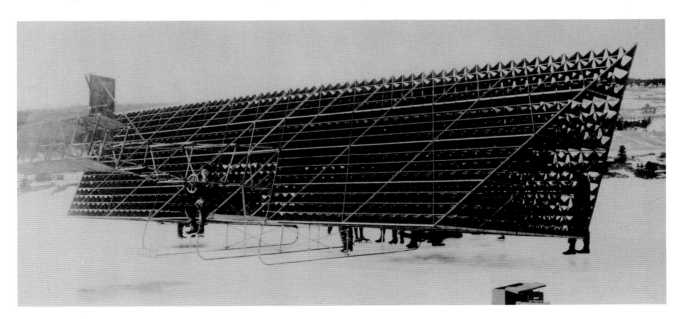

mere 720ft (220m), the flight made by Alberto Santos-Dumont in 14-bis, at Bagatelle in France, was the world's first officially recognized sustained flight, and the first distance record. The Wrights may have been world-famous by now, but their early flights were never officially recognized.

It was nearly five years after the Wrights that another American, Glenn Curtiss, piloting the *June Bug* biplane, flew over 1,266ft (386m), and the following month managed a more impressive 5,088ft (1551m), winning him the *Scientific American* trophy for the first official public flight of over a kilometre (3,280ft).

June Bug wasn't Glenn Curtiss's own machine, but had been developed by the Aerial Experiment Association, which had been founded by Alexander Graham Bell; but Curtiss was adept at winning competitions and prizes and gaining publicity, in contrast with the Wright brothers, who regarded such things as vulgar peepshows, preferring to concentrate on the more serious research in hand. In fact, there had been rivalry between Curtiss and the Wrights, and despite the brothers' undoubted hard work and expertise,

OPPOSITE: The Phillips's Multiplane of 1904 (above) and the more successful 1907 model (below).

BELOW: The Marquis d'Ecquevilly's Multiplane of 1908.

they had begun to fall behind. Orville and Wilbur preferred to work almost secretly on their own, but Curtiss was happy to co-operate with anyone, being quick to spot innovations of which he could make future use. So he

abandoned wing-warping in favour of the far more effective ailerons, and developed wheeled undercarriages to replace skids. By 1909, the Wright brothers had lost what had once been their huge technical lead.

As for the Aerial Experiment Association, the fortunes of its early aircraft had been rather mixed, *Cygnet II* (*page 23*) being one of the strangest, having been devised by Alexander Graham Bell and the pilot J.A.D. McCurdy, and consisting of one large vertical wing, composed of 5,500 tetrahedral cells. There may have been good reasoning behind the design, but when it was tested over the frozen Baddeck Bay in Nova Scotia on 22 February 1909, *Cygnet II* failed to get off the ground. Next day, McCurdy had more luck in a different plane,

successfully achieving Canada's first in *Silver Dart*, another of the association's planes, and flying over 4 miles (6.4km).

Horatio Phillips was wedded to the multi-winged concept and had been building Multiplanes since the 1890s. A steam-powered version was able to fly a short distance, but with a 73-lb (33-kg) weight rather than a pilot, while the manned Multiplane of 1904, with one bank of 20 small wings and a 22-hp engine, was unable to make it off the ground.

Cygnet II had also been based on the concept of using many small wings

BELOW: The Blériot III, seen here in its original floatplane configuration, was an early French machine, built by pioneer aviators Louis Blériot and Gabriel Voisin. It was to be their first design actually to leave the ground under its own power.

OPPOSITE: The Blériot IV in 1906.

to provide lift, rather than two large ones, and the same was true of Horatio Philips's Multiplane of 1907 (*page 24 below*). Built the year before *Cygnet II*, it made the first powered and manned flight in Britain. It had four banks of wings, each comprising 50 narrow-chord surfaces. It may have looked a little like a set of mobile Venetian blinds, but it was a serious contender, powered by a 22-hp engine. Tested at Streatham, in south London, it took off successfully but flew only about 500ft (150m) before touching down. Although Phillips did not continue to build planes, he had clearly demonstrated that flying machines should always have cambered wings.

But Britain and America did not have the monopoly of multi-wings. In France, the Marquis d'Ecquevilly had a machine with 11 wings, built into an

oval-shaped frame surmounted by one more wing (*see page 25*). Some of these wings were dihedral (bent-up) and some anhedral (bent-down), but neither helped the machine to fly, and there is no record that it ever did. Nor were the machine's chances helped by its engine, which was a mere 7 or 8hp; this may have been respectable for a motorcycle at the time, but was not remotely powerful enough to lift man and machine off the ground.

OPPOSITE: The Canard Voisin, developed by Gabriel and Charles Voisin in 1910, its main wings being positioned at the back.

BELOW: Henri Fabre's Hydravion or Le Canard *(The Duck), seen flying in 1910.*

EXPANDING THE ENVELOPE

Despite the elation that had accompanied the Wright brothers' breakthrough back in 1903, little progress was made during the following five years. This was not through want of trying, but the cause had not been helped by Orville and Wilbur's decision to stop flying for three years from 1905. As has been seen, many aeronautical inventors, even in 1908, were still struggling to get off the ground, let alone make sustained, controllable flights. There was still intense interest in

Henri Fabre's Hydravion, the world's first successful powered seaplane, seen off Monaco in 1911.

the concept of powered flight, both from the military as well as the public, and many valuable prizes were being offered to pioneers in return for setting new records.

One such was the £1,000 offered by the *Daily Mail* newspaper to the first pilot to cross the English Channel, which Louis Blériot achieved in his monoplane in July 1909, crash-landing on cliffs near Dover and scooping the prize. The following month, the first International Aviation Meeting was held at Reims in France, where 23 aircraft out of the 38 present flew, watched by thousands and read about in newspapers by millions more.

Meanwhile, the Wright brothers were back in circulation, and on 31 December 1908 Wilbur set a new world distance record of 77.48 miles (124.69km) at Auvours in France. It was quite a feat, when one considers that the Wrights' previous best had been 24 miles, and that they had been absent from flying for three years, yet they would soon be overtaken. The pace of aircraft development was

had been showing an interest in aircraft long before the war. The French War Ministry had commissioned a prototype bomber from Clement Ader (*see page 18*), and despite 1903's pessimistic prediction, the Americans had come round to the idea too; the U.S. Army paid $30,000 for a Wright biplane following a demonstration by the Wrights in 1908. The military had also been active in Britain, its army's balloon facility at Farnborough having been renamed the Royal Aircraft Factory in 1911, when it produced the 60-hp S.E.1, followed by a string of other aircraft, all designed with military objectives in mind.

But the military did not make all the running, and the last few years preceding the First World War saw further developments elsewhere, even though the imperative was still out-and-out performance or experimentation, rather than any commercial concerns; in fact, little thought had been given to the passenger-carrying potential of early aircraft. By this time, however, such a thing as a conventional aircraft did exist, with fixed wings (monoplane or biplane) and a front-mounted engine with a single propeller. But innovators

finally beginning to accelerate, and less than a year after Wilbur set his record it was comprehensively eclipsed by Henri Farman, flying his own biplane over 111 miles (179km). Four years later, another Farman biplane, this time flown by A. Séguin, managed 634 miles (1020m) in one hop; this was over eight times the distance of Wilbur's record, and a measure of how fast aviation technology was advancing.

Conventional wisdom has it that the First World War was the impetus driving technology forward, where the fight for mastery of the skies saw far more resources being poured into improving aircraft performance. The pressures of wartime certainly did force the pace, especially where engine power was concerned, with 200-hp power units producing speeds of well over 100mph (160km/h). But the military were still seeking better solutions, annular wings being a good example. G. Tilghman Richards had built an annular-winged biplane in Britain, in

1911, which did not work well and was destroyed by a winter storm while sitting in its hangar. But the patent for it was acquired by Cedric Lee, who built a successful glider the following year; this had a semi-circular upper wing and a full annular lower. Wind-tunnel tests confirmed the aerodynamic advantage of annular wings; they also needed less wingspan for a given area than conventional wings, while providing a relatively docile stall.

Thus encouraged, Lee built a two-seater annular monoplane in 1913, powered by an 80-hp Gnôme power plant. This fine rotary engine was built in France and was an excellent choice. The French, moreover, had taken an early lead in aviation technology, which they were to maintain up to the war. Unfortunately, this particular Gnôme-powered aircraft proved to be tail-heavy, stalling and crashing on

its first flight. After repair and modification, however, it became a predictable and stable machine, although the annular-wing concept never truly became established. The same was true of the rhomboidal

wing, built by the Edwards company in 1911 and powered by a 50-hp Humber engine driving two large propellers. It was trialled at the Brooklands racetrack in England, but was probably never flown.

THE PURSUIT OF SPEED

Experiments like this were interesting diversions, but no more than that, for the real progress was being made in conventional design. The Deperdussin monoplane was especially advanced,

OPPOSITE: The Batson Flying House, built in 1913.

BELOW: Aleksandr Bezobrazov's fighter triplane of 1914.

being a monocoque design resembling something out of the 1920s rather than 1913, when it was entered for the Gordon Bennett Cup race held at Reims in France. It was low, sleek and

all of a piece, being a world away from the spindly contraptions that had passed for aircraft only a few years before. Powered by the latest 160-hp Gnôme, and with inversely tapering wings to reduce drag, it proved phenomenally fast. That September, piloted by Maurice Prévost, it was the first to break the 200-km/h barrier, reaching 126.666mph (203.84km/h). The Deperdussin monocoque was the

fastest aircraft of its time, even faster than some First World War fighters, but being so oriented toward speed made it less of a practical all-rounder than later single-seaters.

The following year, the Royal Aircraft Factory produced an even faster prototype which, unlike the Deperdussin, did have a military intent, the name S.E.4 standing for 'Scouting Experimental 4'. Like the French

machine, it had a monocoque fuselage and a similar Gnôme engine, being a biplane rather than a monoplane. One innovation, far ahead of its time, was the moulded celluloid cockpit canopy, which was removed when sensitive pilots, used to healthy blasts of fresh air, refused to be boxed in. In 1914, the S.E.4 hit 135mph (217km/h) during trials, but its engine proved unreliable and was replaced by a more modest 100-hp Gnôme Monosoupape; even so, it remained one of the fastest aircraft of its time.

During the First World War, the front-engined monoplane or biplane was possibly seen by many as the standard format, and certainly most of the aircraft produced during the conflict were built along these lines. But there were still some variations on the theme. In Russia, only a few weeks after the Tsarist regime had gone to war with Germany, an army officer, Aleksandr Bezobrazov, flew his new prototype fighter (*page 35*). It was a triplane, not that there was anything special about that, but what made Bezobrazov's machine unique was that the three wings were staggered at an extreme angle: the upper wing was well forward of the fuselage, the middle

was located centrally, and the bottom was almost under the tail section. It never saw active service.

The previous year, fellow Russian Igor Sikorsky's four-engined machine, the first in the world, had flown for the first time. Le Grand, as it was named, would be developed into the Ilya Mourometz biplane, which saw active service as a bomber. At this stage, however, it was difficult to find engines powerful enough to push such a monster along at any speed. The Type B Mourometz had a wingspan of over 100ft (30m) and weighed nearly five tonnes; but it could only stagger along at 60mph (100km/h), even with 670hp from the four Samson Canton-Unnes engines.

But wartime pressures would soon see an escalation in engine power, which meant not only more speed but also faster rates of climb, increased altitude, and larger bomb loads. Fighters became ever faster, and rotary engines, such as the 130-hp Clerget, were used in the Sopwith Camel, while heavier fighters soon left their original reconnaissance role far behind, utilizing bigger inline engines with 200hp or more, making them better suited to aerial dog fights.

Bombers also benefited from the extra horsepower. The Handley Page O/400 of 1918, for example, had about the same wingspan as the Russian Mourometz, and two 360-hp Rolls-Royce Eagles made it only slightly more powerful, yet it was capable of reaching 97mph (156km/h) with a massive bomb load of 1,000lbs (454kg) on board. A far lighter British bomber was the De Havilland DH4, with its mere 458-lb (208-kg) payload; but its single 375-hp Eagle was able to propel it at 143mph (230km/h), making it faster than many fighters. Italy also built multi-engined bombers, notable among which were the Capronis.

But the Germans certainly put more effort into developing heavy bombers than any other nation, which probably stemmed from their long tradition as airship pioneers, some of which bombed London and the English coast. The Zeppelin-Staaken R VI was the largest aircraft to see active service during the war. Its wingspan was over 138ft (42m), but it was not over-engined, its four 245-hp Maybach or 260-hp Mercedes units limiting speed to 84mph (135km/h), and with a bomb load no bigger

The Ilya Mourometz biplane saw active service as a bomber during the First World War.

than that of the Handley Page. The same lack of power also hampered the Gotha and Friedrichshafen heavy bombers, each of which was equipped with only two 260-hp Mercedes power units.

All of these were relatively conventional machines, but the Linke-Hofmann R1 was rather different, being one of the most unconventional bombers of the war. A biplane, it had been developed in a wind tunnel, where experiments indicated that expanding the fuselage to fill the interplane gap would have lift-to-drag ratio benefits. The pilot sat above the entire edifice, which could make landing difficult, while the fuselage space was used to house four Mercedes D IV engines driving two large propellers. After the war, new research confirmed these early experiments to have been feasible, which did nothing to help the R1, whose first protoype broke up in mid-air, the second flipping over while landing, and which served to hasten the RI's eventual abandonment.

WEIRD AIRCRAFT

OPPOSITE ABOVE: The Sopwith Bat Boat, some of which were supplied to Germany before 1914.

OPPOSITE BELOW: The SPAD A.4, some ten of which were produced and sold to Russia.

BELOW: The Armstrong Whitworth F.K.12 in its prototype form.

The First World War proved the aircraft's military potential as a fighter, a reconnaissance plane, and as a heavy bomber. The bombers, in particular, had been the new face of industrial warfare, and even though these early machines were at times inaccurate and inflicted little real damage, they were effective in keeping men and their guns, who might otherwise be shelling the trenches, occupied. And although most of the wartime developments consisted of increasing engine power, many others involved new innovations. Some of these may have been technical dead-ends, but they demonstrated that even though the pioneering days of flight were drawing to a close, there was still a very real need for truly innovative aircraft.

CHAPTER TWO
PEOPLE-CARRIERS, PIGGYBACKS & SPEED

The First World War not only established the aircraft's credentials as a military machine but also proved it could be mass-produced, and that it could be reliable and carry heavy payloads at relatively high speeds. But this didn't mean that manufacturers could expect immediate peacetime dividends by turning their attention to building freight- and passenger-carrying machines.

For one thing, the end of wartime production had been abrupt. Thousands of aircraft were built in 1918 alone, and the vast majority of them were now surplus to requirements. In 1919, Europe needed essentials, such as food and housing, rather than high-

BELOW: The Handley Page W8 (also known as the H.P.18) was the company's first civil transport aircraft.

OPPOSITE: The Caproni Ca. 60 was a mere prototype for a 150-seater designed for transatlantic flight. It made a short flight in March 1921 over Lake Maggiore, in Italy, before crashing and breaking up.

speed fighters and bombers. So they were stockpiled and gradually sold off, some of them in unopened crates at rockbottom prices. The air forces were rapidly disbanded, and within a year of the November 1918 armistice, the Royal Air Force had been pared down from 188 operational squadrons to only 12.

Aircraft manufacturers, having only recently been urged to produce as many machines as possible, now faced abrupt cancellations of orders, with some turning their attention to making alternative products, such as buses, motorcycles or even sheds in order to survive, while others closed down completely. A few managed to stay in business, facing a shrunken market which now had very different needs.

There was an obvious potential for aircraft in which people and freight could be moved around, and at previously undreamt of speeds, but the market for them was small. Airmail services began in the U.S. in 1918, expanding gradually through the 1920s and '30s while being only a tiny proportion of the total, while passenger air travel was even slower to get going.

Ships, trains and cars were becoming faster and more luxurious by the year, while flying was still regarded as a more dangerous form of transport. Passengers shivered in unheated, cramped and unpressurized cabins, deafened by engine noise and shaken by constant vibrations. Air sickness was found to be just as unpleasant as its equivalent at sea, and pressure on the ears caused problems during take-offs and landings. Even in 1934, which was one of the most popular interwar years for passenger flights in America, flying made up less than 2 per cent of all intercity journeys, while in Europe, with a less affluent population and shorter distances, the corresponding figure would have undoubtedly been even less.

In spite of this, nascent passenger air services were a feature of the early 1920s. Aéropostale in France, Lufthansa in Germany, and Britain's Imperial Airways, the latter government-subsidized and with a brief to develop air links with the Empire as well as Europe, were all established for much the same reasons. The planes that were used at first were modified bombers: the Handley Page W8 'flying saloon', for example, having been based on the company's wartime heavyweights, and which could carry 15–20 passengers or a respectable amount of freight. The situation was more difficult in Germany, where the Treaty of Versailles had severely restricted the types of aircraft the country was permitted to build, although Junkers was able to convert its wartime J10 into the peacetime F13. This was an advanced machine, and

was the world's first all-metal airliner to enter service, being a monoplane with low-mounted cantilevered wings. The treaty, however, stipulated that it could carry only two crew and four passengers, and it would be ten years before Germany had a giant airliner of its own.

THE FIRST AIRLINERS

Today, most airliners are based on the same principle of a passenger-carrying fuselage and wheeled undercarriage, but when new designs began to appear in the 1920s, a degree of lateral thinking went into their design, producing a variety of aircraft that simply look odd to 21st-century eyes. Passengers were housed in broad 'lifting-body' fuselages, in the nose-cone, and even in the wings. In the absence of suitable airfields and the need for making emergency landings when flying over water, flying boats came to have something of a heyday. The problem of range was addressed in various ways, with piggyback launches and economical diesel-powered planes. Aircraft got ever larger, culminating in Howard Hughes's 181-tonne *Spruce Goose*.

Several of these elements were combined in the Caproni Ca. 60 Triple

The Burnelli UB-14 'Red Devil' of 1934.

Hydro-Triplane (*page 41*). Caproni, of course, had produced multi-engined bombers for Italy's war effort, and quickly began adapting them for carrying passengers once peacetime had arrived. One triplane prototype was able to carry 23 fare-payers, and in 1920 there was a much larger five-engined machine able to carry 30 people, with 110-ft (33.5-m) wingspans. But both of these were dwarfed by the Ca. 60 which, quite simply, was a giant.

Carrying 100 passengers, it had eight 400-hp Liberty power units, arranged in both tractor and pusher positions. The three tandem sets of triplane wings had no conventional elevators, and longitudinal control was provided by opposed deflection of the ailerons in the front and rearmost wings, or at least, that was the theory; but in practice it did not work too well. Incredibly, the Ca. 60 was intended to be a model of an even larger machine intended for transatlantic flights.

Naturally, it was a flying boat, and the prototype was floated out onto Lake Maggiore in February 1921 for extensive trials. These went well, and

the plane made its first flight early the following month, covering about a mile before touching down on the waters of the lake. Alas, a second flight two days later ended with an unplanned dive into the water, damaging the hull so badly that the whole project had to be abandoned.

There was nothing innovative about the Caproni Ca. 60, apart from its sheer size, and many of the early post-war airliners relied more on engine power than on aerodynamic sophistication. But in America, just as the giant Caproni was lumbering across Lake Maggiore, another manufacturer was planning something far more advanced; none of the Remington-Burnelli Aircraft Corporation's advanced passenger planes met with commercial success during the 1920s, but they pointed the way toward a new appreciation of aerodynamics.

The first of these was the distinctive RB1, its fuselage resembling a thick aerofoil section, which was no accident since it was intended to be just that. It was given an aerofoil shape to make it slip through the air more easily than a traditional squared-off fuselage,

and it was broad so as to increase lift. To further aid aerodynamics, the two 420-hp Liberty engines were hidden inside the nose, rather than in separate nacelles. The two crew members still sat in an open cockpit, but the 25 passengers had plenty of space in the 14-ft (4-m) wide fuselage, which had a corrugated duralumin skin over a plywood frame for added strength.

In practice, the RB1 had its flaws: squeezing both engines into the nose meant that the propeller hubs were little more than 10ft apart, thus reducing the props' effectiveness, and the tail's efficiency was compromised by the aerofoil shape of the fuselage. A freight-only RB2 showed some improvements, however, having been given a tapered rear fuselage to improve the tail, duralumin-covered wings, and 520-hp Galloway Atlantic engines; but the Remington-Burnelli still failed to attract customers.

Not to be deterred, company boss, Vincent Burnelli, persevered with his avant-garde airliners, his next project being the CB-16 of 1927. Like its predecessor, it was relatively small, in that it was able to carry only 20 passengers, but its twin 625-hp Curtiss Conquerers made it rather more

The Remington-Burnelli RB1 airliner.

powerful. Unlike the RB1, it was a monoplane, and had the further modern feature of a retractable undercarriage, which could be crank-operated from the cockpit. The CB-16 was able to top 150mph (240km/h), and was followed by a smaller version, the GX-3, with two 90-hp engines and a variable-camber monoplane wing.

Burnelli was a constant innovator, never to be satisfied with what was currently in production. So alongside the 1929 GX-3 came a modified version of the CB-16, the UB-20, which featured stressed metal skin and 800-hp Packard engines, though it also reverted to a fixed undercarriage. As with the entire series, the UB-20 had a lifting-body fuselage, designed to contribute to lift, and the same was true of the radical UB-14 (*page 43*) that followed in 1934.

As the number suggests, this was a smaller plane than the first UB, with space for only 14 passengers and with less powerful 680-hp Pratt & Whitney units. But for the first time it provided an enclosed cockpit for the crew; the fuselage was wide and short, acting as the centre section of the monoplane wings. It was connected to a twin tail by

two booms, that were effectively extensions of the fin area. Unlike earlier Remington-Burnellis, the two Pratt & Whitney radial engines were not squeezed into the nose, although they had fairings to minimize the aerodynamic disruption.

The UB-14 was a forward-looking, highly promising small airliner, but like its predecessors was not a commercial success. The prototype suffered damage while landing in 1935, and although an improved successor, the UB-14B, was developed, this too came to nothing. A deal was signed for Cunliffe Owen Aircraft to build it in Britain from 1937,

powered by 710-hp Bristol Perseus engines, but only one ever came to fruition. The same fate befell the CBY-3 Loadmaster, the last of Burnelli's lifting-body designs, with a similar aerofoil-shaped fuselage, twin-boom tail, and two 1450-hp Pratt & Whitney Twin Wasps. A plan for its manufacture in Canada by the Cancargo Aircraft Manufacturing Company failed to materialize. The prototype survived, however, as a testament to the far-sightedness of Vincent Burnelli.

But he did not have a monopoly of the concept of a lifting fuselage, and Dyle et Bacalan, in France, built a

whole series of aircraft based around the idea in the 1920s and early '30s. Once again, there was no commercial success, though all were monoplanes with twin-boom tails. The DB10 night bomber was the first, carrying its twin engines close together in similar fashion to the Burnelli RB. The triple-engined DB70 (tested from 1929) and DB71 airliners, and the AB20 and AB21 bombers, all sprang from the same line, having a fuselage nacelle ahead of the main lifting-body section.

The airliners had two cabins, one in each boom, each big enough for ten people, plus a saloon for eight more in the centre section. Interestingly, even their bomber cousins had glazed leading edges in the thick fuselage section, but with the addition of a gun turret. Although the French army requisitioned a DB70 to carry troops on manoeuvres in 1931, this series of aircraft made no further progress beyond the prototypes.

The same could not be said of the Junkers G38, which actually made it into production, albeit to a limited extent. By 1929, Germany was permitted to build larger aircraft, and the G38 certainly fitted that description. The wingspan was 144ft 4in (44m), but it was the size and shape of the wings that was the big Junkers's

OPPOSITE: The Dyle et Bacalan DB70 airliner, tested from 1929.

BELOW: The giant Junkers G38 airliner with its wing cabins.

most important innovation. The span and chord-width made the wings deep enough to accommodate a three-

passenger cabin on either side, allowing its occupants to peer out of the glazed sections, while another lucky two were tucked into the nose, with an unparalleled view that can only be imagined by jet airliner passengers, leaving a further 26 to be seated more conventionally in the main fuselage. Four 750-hp engines powered the G38,

which made its maiden flight in November 1929. In the end, only two were made, both carrying paying passengers. They were operated by Deutsche Lufthansa.

Another facet of the G38 story was that Mitsubishi of Japan bought a licence to build it, and made six in the early 1930s, modified as heavy bombers

in the hope that the resulting Ki-20 would have sufficient range to attack the Philippines; but in the event, none of them saw active service.

Whether they be tractors, ships or tanks, the Soviet Union liked to build

The Soviet Tupolev ANT-20MG Maxim Gorki.

48

them big, and the same applied to aircraft. The Kalunin K-7 had a wingspan of nearly 174ft (53m), and it was the wing that was its unique feature. It was elliptical, with a huge chord of nearly 35ft (11m) allowing a maximum depth of 7ft 8in (2.3m). The reason for these massive dimensions was that the aircraft was originally envisaged as an airliner, with its entire 120-passenger load carried inside what was very nearly a flying wing. Twin tailbooms supported a large elliptical tail and the cockpit nacelle was built onto the wing's leading edge.

If all this had come to pass, the K-7 would undoubtedly have spent its working life ferrying Communist party officials across the Soviet empire, from Vladivostock to the Ukraine, but it never happened. Suspicious of Western intentions, Stalin led the Soviets through a massive rearmament programme in the 1930s, so that when the K-7 began to take shape in 1931 it was as a heavy bomber. In terms of pure payload it was well-suited to the role: a total of seven M-34F engines (six tractor and one pusher) allowed it a standard bomb payload of 14.5 tonnes, or 19 tonnes in overload. Fully laden, with the addition of defensive guns, the gargantuan K-7

weighed up to 42 tonnes while still managing 140mph (225km/h). But development was swiftly abandoned when a tailboom failed at low altitude and the K-7 crashed, killing all but five of the 20 crew on board. Two other K-7s, that were currently under construction, were also abandoned.

The K-7 may have been big, but it wasn't by any means the largest land-based aircraft of its time. That title went to another Soviet machine, the Tupolev ANT-20MG Maxim Gorki, named after the great Russian-Soviet writer. Despite its size, it was intended to be neither a super-airliner nor a super-heavy bomber. Instead, the plane was to be the ultimate propaganda machine. A natural for state occasions and air parades, it had spotlights on its undercarriage to illuminate rousing messages displayed on the wing undersides. Inside, rather than being packed with seats or high explosives, the Maxim Gorki came equipped with printing equipment, radios, a photographic laboratory and film projectors, and there was even a powerful external radio set, referred to as the 'voice in the sky'.

Tupolev, of course, was a well-established builder of large aircraft. Its TB-1 and TB-3 heavy bombers were

Soviet standard equipment, and were still in use, both as transport planes and as bombers, when Operation Barbarossa set the Nazi war machine rolling into the U.S.S.R. Like its predecessors, the Maxim Gorki was a monoplane, though with a 206-ft (63-m) wingspan. Even unladen it weighed 28.5 tonnes, and needed all of its eight 900-hp Mikulin M-34 FRN engines. Six of these were mounted directly on the wings, with the other two in tandem mounted on struts on top of the main fuselage. These were enough to give the Gorky a ceiling height of nearly 15,000ft (4572m), but despite a range of 1,200 miles (1930km), the aircraft was designed to be disassembled and transported by rail, should the need arise.

Many of the aircraft featured here met their end on test flights, but the Maxim Gorki would appear to have been simply unlucky. It was completed in April 1934, and in May the following year was performing a demonstation pass over Moscow, escorted by three fighters. One of these, a Polikarpov I-5, piloted by Nikolai Blagin, attempted a loop around the huge plane's wings. He miscalculated, hit the wing, and both planes plunged to the ground, killing Blagin and 45 on board the Maxim

Gorki, some of them the relatives of engineers who had worked on the plane. While the authorities pronounced the fatal manoeuvre to have been impromptu and reckless, it has been suggested that it might have been a planned part of the show. Either way, the word Blaginism entered the Russian vocabulary to describe a 'cocky disregard for authority'.

As had happened so often before, a crash put a stop to the project, which included plans for another 16 Maxim Gorkis. Instead, it was redesigned as the smaller, six-engined ANT-20bis, being a genuine airliner that could carry up to 85 passengers. The first one was completed in 1938, and in 1940 was still operating a service between Moscow and Mineralnye Vody. No more were built, and the plane was destroyed in 1942.

FLYING & FLOATING

Flying boats are evocative of a golden age of flying, when rich trend-setters landed on the smooth waters of exotic lagoons, far from the hectic bustle of landlocked airports. Yet there were good practical reasons for their existence in the interwar period. Most were designed to fly long distances,

The Latécoère 521, a French six-engined flying boat, and one of the first of the large transatlantic passenger aircraft.

which usually meant travelling over water. Given the minimal navigational aids of the time, and the less than perfect reliability, the ability to touch down and take off from any sizeable stretch of calmish water was an excellent safety feature. Moreover, there were few runways long enough to accommodate large wheeled aircraft at that time.

Although small and medium-sized flying boats were built in larger numbers, such as the successful Boeing 314, these giant machines hold an undeniable fascination. France may have lost its early-century lead in aviation, but it was still a prolific builder of such aircraft, in this case the Latécoère 521, a six-engined monster with a wingspan only three inches short of 162ft (50m). Intended largely for trans-Mediterranean flight, it was also capable of crossing the Atlantic (albeit with a passenger rating reduced from 70 to 30).

The Latécoère 521 sank at its moorings in Miami, while on a circuit of the Atlantic, but apart from that episode was a huge success. A sister 522 followed, and both were requisitioned by the French navy on the outbreak of the Second World War, although the 522 was soon allowed to resume passenger operations. Three more Latécoère 523s were built to military specifications and were able to patrol the Atlantic for up to 33 hours at a time. Sadly, none of these survived the war.

Latécoère had been building the even larger 188-ft (57-m) wingspan 631, even before Hitler invaded Poland and France, which was designed to transport 40 passengers across the Atlantic. Nine were built after the war, some with 1600-hp Wright radial engines, making the dream of a regular transatlantic service a reality. The dream was short-lived, however, for two

OPPOSITE: The Dornier Do X, the largest flying boat of the interwar years, its Bristol Jupiter engines arranged in six tandem pairs.

RIGHT: The Tupolev ANT-22 (MK-1) twin-hulled flying boat.

planes were lost within a year, after which the 631s were restricted to freight duties for a while before being left to lie idle in their hangars.

But the idea of a regular transatlantic service remained a seductive one, especially for manufacturers and airlines with ambitions to beat the great Blue Riband ocean liners at their own game, and this certainly was the thinking behind the Dornier Do X, the biggest and heaviest flying boat to be built between the wars. Alongside hopes of a regular airship service between Europe and America, the Do X was designed to carry between 40 and 80 passengers, although there was actually room for 150 within its spacious hull, as well as ten crew and (on one occasion) nine crafty stowaways. This would have

been luxury travel indeed, with only 40 privileged passengers sharing all that space.

The Do X dwarfed almost every dimension of other aircraft. It was 28-ft (8.5-m) longer than the Latécoère 521, and its maximum take-off weight was half as much again. It required 12 525-hp Bristol Jupiter engines (later 600-hp Curtiss Conquerers) and had a

top speed of 134mph (216km/h). But even that much power could not exceed a ceiling of 1,640ft (500m), and with a range of 1,050 miles (1690km), the Do X had to make its Atlantic crossing in stages. Guzzling 350 gallons of fuel an hour, the biggest-ever Dornier sadly proved to be impracticable.

The Soviets naturally had a giant flying boat of their own, the Tupolev

ANT-22 (*page 53*), which began trials in 1934. It resembled no other aircraft, its twin massive hulls joined by a thick centre-section wing, as if two large aircraft had been simply welded together. Being a Soviet plane, it was not intended to ferry rich capitalists across the Atlantic, but was envisaged as a reconnaissance-bomber, with a six-tonne bomb load and no less than six gun turrets. In tests, this giant Tupolev proved quite seaworthy but was otherwise a disappointment, and the project was abandoned in 1936.

But the Tupolevs, the Latécoères and Dorniers seemed like toys compared with the infamous *Spruce Goose*, which had the longest wingspan of all time. The original impetus for the flying boat came, not from the flamboyant billionaire Howard Hughes, but from the U.S. Navy, which in 1942 laid down the specification for an extra-large craft, capable of swallowing up to 700 troops and big enough to carry two 30-tonne tanks. The sting in the tail

ABOVE: The twin-hulled Savoia-Marchetti S.66 flying boat.

OPPOSITE: The Blériot 5190 'Santos-Dumont', a large parasol-wing monoplane flying boat.

was that it had to be made of wood, the reason being that wartime metal shortages were anticipated.

Typically, when the government pulled the plug on the project, Howard Hughes decided to carry on and finish the plane on his own, being probably the only man in the world with the experience, the determination, and the dollars to do so. Nevertheless, it was a daunting project, and Hughes teamed up with shipbuilder Henry Kaiser to complete the project. Perhaps inevitably, the Hughes H-4 Hercules, to give it its official title, turned out to be overweight and out-of-time, and Hughes is rumoured to have wasted $22 million of his own money in the process.

The war was long over by the time the 181-tonne *Spruce Goose* was finally floated in Los Angeles harbour for its first trial in 1947. With Hughes himself at the controls, the eight 3000-hp Pratt & Whitneys powered the huge plane on its first taxi run. On the second, however, it seemed unexpectedly buoyant, and Hughes used the third run to attempt an unscheduled flight. The *Spruce Goose* duly took off, admittedly flying only a mile or so at an altitude of

75ft (23m), but fly it did. Perhaps Hughes was merely proving a point, for the *Spruce Goose* never attempted to taxi again, let alone fly, and now sits in

Oregon's Evergreen Aviation Museum as an awe-inspiring exhibit.

But the days of the flying boat were drawing to a close, even as *Spruce*

Goose was making its one and only flight. An after-effect of the war was that many more concrete runways were being made available on ex-military

OPPOSITE: The Felixstowe Fury (Porte Sugar Baby), designed by John Cyril Porte of the Seaplane Experimental Station, Felixstowe, England.

BELOW, PAGES 58 & 59: Howard Hughes's H-4 Hercules (Spruce Goose), seen below and subsequently at Oregon's Evergreen Aviation Museum.

bases all over the world, and as had been the case after the First World War, huge numbers of ex-service aircraft were up for grabs at relatively modest prices. The difference, this time, was that planes like the ex-U.S.A.F. Douglas Dakota were eminently suitable for post-war use, either for carrying passengers or for freight. In fact, there was little need of a flying boat when

such a cheap and durable aircraft as the Dakota could fly from more convenient airports close to city centres.

Perhaps the last of the old-school flying boats was the elegantly-named Saunders-Roe Princess (*page 61*), conceived in the midst of war as a civilian machine with the ability to carry up to 220 people across the Atlantic non-stop, which was

something that had eluded previous craft. The go-ahead was given in 1945 by the Ministry of Supply and the BOAC airline, though they were to withdraw from the project. This didn't necessarily mean the end of the Princess, however, which still had potential as a military freight-carrier for the RAF, so work continued.

The finished plane was impressive, with its 219-ft (67-m) wingspan and ten Bristol Proteus 2 turboprop engines, each one delivering 3780hp. Eight of these were in coupled pairs, the other two mounted individually. The Princess first flew in August 1952 and made 47 flights over the next two years; these were mostly of a short duration,

and it amassed only 97 hours of flying time. By 1954, the project was dead, and the completed and half-finished Princesses were mothballed for over a decade against a hoped-for sale which never materialized. In a sad end to a graceful era, the Princess was eventually bought by a breaker, who decided to use part of its massive hull as office space.

PEOPLE-CARRIERS, PIGGYBACKS & SPEED

There were still flying boats in the years that followed, of course, mainly for military use, such as the jet-powered Russian-made Beriev. More unusual, however, was the amphibious Beriev VVA-14, that first flew in August 1972.

It was designed by Robert Bartini in answer to a perceived requirement to destroy U.S. Navy Polaris missile submarines, and was able to float on two large pontoons attached to the deep centre-section wing. The VVA-14

appeared to be an adaptable aircraft, and with its 12 RD-36 lift-jets, as well as the two turbofan engines, was expected to make not only vertical take-offs, but also short take-offs and landings on both land and water.

IN SEARCH OF RANGE

The range of aircraft, determined by fuel capacity, is a perennial problem, the obvious solution being to fit a larger fuel tank or tanks. But some more inventive methods were also tried that are perhaps of greater interest. In-flight refuelling is regarded as a modern procedure, but Imperial Airways made successful experiments based on the concept in 1939. It was seeking a way of flying non-stop across the Atlantic,

and to this end modified a Caribou
flying boat to accept refuelling on the
move. It took off from Southampton
on 5 August, and after being
replenished by a Handley Page Harrow
tanker aircraft, carried on to New York
via Foynes, Botwood and Montreal. A
series of refuelled flights followed,
though in the same year, the new
Boeing 314 flying boat made a non-
stop run from New York to Lisbon
without refuelling.

The alternative was to find an
engine that simply used less fuel and
that could go further on the same
amount. Before the escalation in oil
prices in 2008, diesel engines were again
beginning to find favour for small
private planes, due to their fuel
efficiency, but this wasn't a new idea.
Diesel engines had been used in the
Hindenburg, *Graf Zeppelin* and R101
airships, and between the wars Bristol
had produced a diesel version of its
Pegasus nine-cylinder radial. Named
the Phoenix, this was fitted to a
Westland Wapiti biplane and
performed well, setting an altitude

*The Short-Mayo Composite, a piggyback
long-range seaplane-flying boat
combination produced by Short Brothers.*

Zveno was a parasite aircraft project developed in the Soviet Union during the 1930s, which in this case has a Tupolev TB-3 heavy bomber acting as a mothership for three Polikarpov 1-5 fighters. (See page 68 et seq.)

record of 27,453ft (8368m) in May 1934. Meanwhile, in the U.S.A., Packard was also producing a diesel version of one of its radials, which was able to set an endurance record powering a small Bellanca, of 84 hours and 32 minutes non-stop.

Germany has always been a leader in diesel technology, and naturally it contributed to the development of diesel aircraft. In fact, the Junkers Jumo was probably the most successful diesel aero-engine of all time, being an opposed-piston supercharged two-stroke that was also made under licence by Napier in Britain and by CLM in France. The Junkers Ju86 bomber was actually designed around the Jumo 205, in that it was intended to make use of its long-range capabilities for long-distance missions. In production from 1935, the

diesel-powered Ju 86 (the plane was also offered with petrol power) proved unreliable during the Spanish Civil War, but a later high-altitude version was most successful. A modified Ju86, with pressurized cabin, was capable of reaching nearly 40,000ft (12295m), and was used for high-level reconnaissance out of reach of the standard Allied fighters. A later version, with a 1500-hp Jumo 208, raised its ceiling to 47,250ft (14400m).

But the Jumo was also put to a more peaceful use: Germany was keen

to instigate a regular transatlantic mail service, and chose the Dornier Do 18 for the job. This smooth-looking flying boat was the successor to the highly successful Dornier Wal, a high-winged monoplane that first flew in March 1935. Powered by twin 540-hp Jumo 5s, it could cruise at 135mph (217km/h). Two years later, a modified Do 18F, fitted with two 600-hp Jumo 205C engines, set a new non-stop seaplane record of 5,214 miles (8390km) between Britain and Brazil, making the trip in 43 hours. Meanwhile, Lufthansa had begun its weekly mail service across the South Atlantic, catapult-launching aircraft from ships to extend their range. After the war, Napier designed the Nomad, a 3125-hp two-stroke diesel which was also a compound engine. But it never flew, for the days of complex high-powered piston engines in aircraft were rapidly coming to a close.

There was in any case another means of dramatically extending the range of smaller aircraft, which was to 'piggyback' them on top of larger machines and launch them from there.

Zveno-2 experiments with a Tupolev TB-3 motherplane, overwing Polikarpov I-5s, underwing Polikarpov 1-6s, and a central Grigorovich using a hook-on retrieval system.

Any aircraft could maintain flight at a higher weight than that at which it could take off, and this method allowed it to start its flight in mid-air, with a full load of fuel and cargo. Major R.H. Mayo actually patented this system for what he termed a 'composite aircraft', and it was adopted by Shorts, which

built the Short-Mayo Composite (*pages 62–63*), consisting of an S20 seaplane carried by an Empire flying boat. These two (named the *Mercury* and *Maia* respectively) made a coupled flight in January 1938 and the first in-flight launch of *Mercury* the following month. In July, a combined take-off was made by them from Foynes, in Ireland, after which they separated and *Mercury* continued on to Montreal, in Canada, carrying 1,000lbs (454kg) of newspapers and photographs. It was the first-ever commercial load to be carried non-stop across the Atlantic by aircraft. The *Mercury/Maia* composite went on to make many more flights, including one from Scotland to South Africa, setting a new non-stop seaplane record of 5,997 miles (9651km) in the process, and was operating a regular

66

OPPOSITE: A Convair BR-36.

BELOW: A Convair B-36 and Republic F.84F Thunderstreak, initially the YF-96A parasite fighter.

Southampton–Alexandria service at the outbreak of war.

The coming of war inevitably brought the military potential of piggyback launches to the fore. But the Luftwaffe's Mistel programme was less concerned with extending range than with delivering an unmanned bomber, packed full of high explosive direct to its target. A manned fighter (a Messerschmitt Bf 109 on the first operational unit) was mounted on top

RIGHT & OPPOSITE ABOVE & BELOW: The McDonnell XF-85 Goblin, a fighter aircraft conceived during the Second World War and intended to be carried in the bomb bay of the giant Convair B-36 bomber as a defensive parasite fighter. It was nicknamed the 'Flying Egg' on account of its small and rotund appearance.

of an unmanned multi-engined bomber, following which the fighter pilot would fly both to the target and release the bomber when he was sure it was on course for the final approach. The first Mistel operation was targeted against Allied shipping, supporting D-Day in the Seine Bay. Five composites attacked, each bomber with a 3,800-lb (1725-kg) warhead in the nose. It wasn't an ideal solution, however, and problems concerning pilot guidance were brought to the fore.

The Soviets had been experimenting with composites since the late 1920s. The project was named Zveno (*see pages 64 and 65*), and it was the brainchild of the designer Vladimir Vakhmistrov, who reasoned that a heavy bomber could carry fighters for its own protection, to be released when needed. Experiments with gliders

symmetrically to avoid uneven loadings. The bomber pilot also had the difficult job of keeping as straight and as level as possible while the launches were in process.

The concept of a parasite fighter, carried by the bomber it was intended to protect, was adopted by the Americans after the war, in this case using the Convair B-36 intercontinental strategic bomber. Instead of adapting an existing fighter, McDonnell built one specifically designed for mid-air launch – the XF-85 Goblin – an extraordinary little aircraft with a tiny wingspan of 21ft 3in (6.5m) and a length of less than 15ft (4.5m); it was small enough to squeeze into the bomb

encouraged Tupolev to persevere, and the first Zveno set-up involved a TB-1 bomber with Tupolev I-4 fighters launched from its wings. The larger Tupolev TB-3 'mothership' bomber proved even more suitable, in that it was able to carry three of the larger I-5 fighters, and finally five planes in all: two above and below each wing, plus a fifth attached to a hook retrieval system. In practice, the TB-3 proved to be unwieldy with a full complement of five fighters, which had to be released

bay of the B-36, as long as its wings were folded up. At launch time, it was lowered from the bay on a retractable trapeze and was then let go; the trapeze would also retrieve the Goblin once its mission had been completed.

This may seem straightforward, but the manoeuvre proved extremely tricky, in that the Goblin's small size made it difficult to control it with

finesse, athough it was later improved with the addition of fins to the wingtips. But the little machine was no ordinary prop-driven plane and in the jet age was powered by a Westinghouse J34-WE-22 turbojet, delivering 3,000lbs of thrust, enough to produce 520mph (835km/h).

In August 1948, carried by a modified B-29 bomber, the Goblin

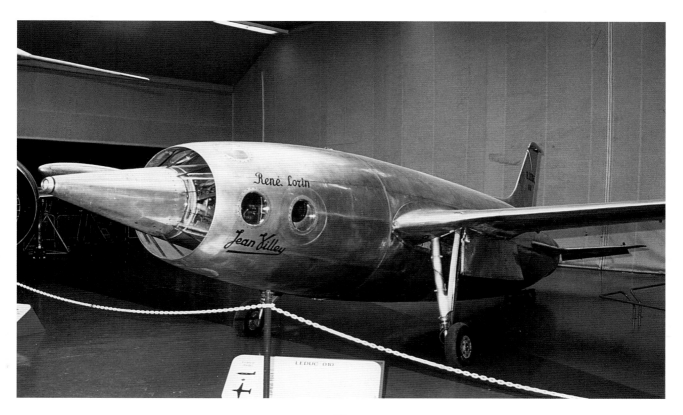

made its first mid-air launch from a trapeze in an operation that was completed without incident; it was when hooking it back onto the trapeze that things began to go wrong. Turbulence and the Goblin's innate

The Leduc ramjet 010-01 (above) and atop a Languedoc 31 airliner (opposite).

instability made a difficult task near-impossible, and as it approached for another attempt, its canopy struck the trapeze so hard that the covering shattered, ripping off the pilot's helmet and oxygen mask in the process. Fortunately, the pilot was experienced and the Goblin had been equipped with landing skids, just in case; by

sucking on the oxygen tube, the pilot was able to keep on flying and make an emergency landing at 170mph (275km/h).

Later, after the Goblin's stability had been improved by additional wingtip fins, it was successfully launched and retrieved several times later in the year, though it was never

BELOW & OPPOSITE: The Space Shuttle Enterprise *atop a Boeing 747.*

used by operational B-36s. France was also making mid-air launches around this time, although the Leduc ramjet, launched from the top of a Languedoc airliner, was a purely experimental aircraft rather than a fighter.

The Americans had originally intended that their Space Shuttle be piggybacked into the sky on top of a modified Boeing 747. A shuttle was carried in this way during early aerodynamic tests, and in August 1977 was actually launched from the back of the 747 for gliding tests back to earth. For the actual space missions, however, the shuttle was vertically launched from the ground. But the Russians utilized this concept throughout, launching their Buran

OPPOSITE: The Buran space orbiter atop an Antonov An-225 freightliner.

BELOW: The Airbus A380 was launched in 2007 and is claimed to be the largest passenger airliner in the world.

space orbiter from the back of an Antonov An-225 Mriya freighter.

The An-225 had been designed specifically for the task, and is in itself an incredible aircraft. Powered by six turbofan engines, it is the largest aircraft ever built, having a 289-ft (88-m) wingspan and an overall length of 275ft (84m), making it as long as an English football pitch. Designed to carry massive loads, the maximum specified was 250 tonnes, or about twice that of a Boeing 747, while fully laden it could easily tip the scales at 450 tonnes.

When the Airbus A380 was launched in 2007, it too was widely claimed to be the largest aircraft in the world, despite being 36ft (11m) shorter and offering 26ft (8m) less wingspan. What is undeniable, however, is that it is the largest passenger aircraft ever built, capable of holding up to 840 people. The An-225 was mothballed when the Buran space programme came to an end in 1994, but was later

returned to service as a specialist
freighter for one-off ultra-large loads.

IN SEARCH OF SPEED

If one examines the history of any
form of transport, be it powered by
humans, animals or the internal
combustion engine, it will be apparent
that somebody, somewhere, has striven
to make it go faster. Cars, bicycles,
motorcycles and trains – all have their
enthusiasts where speed is concerned,
and the same goes for aircraft.

But the pursuit of speed does have
some practical benefits. The aircraft
described here may have been totally
impractical for carrying freight or
people, but the single-minded approach
of their creators did much to extend the
boundaries of knowledge, particularly
where aerodynamics was concerned.

Once it became clear that
sustained, controlled powered flight
was a reality, the speed contests soon
followed, beginning in earnest after the
First World War. At first, modified

fighters were the obvious choice as
speedsters, being the fastest craft of
their time, and the Deutsch de la
Meurthe Cup of 1919 was dominated
by such as these, the SPAD XX and
Nieuport-Delage 29 being particularly
prominent in that event.

In fact, the Blériot SPAD was also
an excellent example of one of these.
Launched too late to take part in the
hostilities, its speed potential was soon
realized, thanks in part to its 300-hp
Hispano-Suiza engine. It was able to set

a new world speed record, even in 1918, for a two-seater aircraft at 143mph (230km/h), and the following year added an altitude record of 29,200ft (8900m). Racers then found that by reducing the wingspan they could increase speed, and the XX gained miles per hour, year on year, achieving 157mph (253km/h) by October 1919. Within another year, Bernard de Romanet had flown a SPAD XX to take the absolute world record, at a speed of 182mph, then 193mph (311km/h).

In September 1920, the Gordon Bennett Aviation Cup race was held at Étampes in France, when it was won by a Nieuport-Delage 29v. The fact that it had been held in France, and that a French machine had won the race (the SPAD was also French), reflected that nation's early lead in aviation, but another plane at Étampes was even

OPPOSITE: The Dayton-Wright RB racer at Étampes in 1920. It was developed for the 1920 Gordon Bennett race, and was perhaps one of the most advanced concepts developed at that time.

RIGHT: A Stipa monoplane with Venturi duct fuselage.

more significant, in that, among other things, it was an American craft.

The Dayton-Wright RB was innovative in several ways, as one would have expected from a company that had Orville Wright as its consulting engineer. Orville's brother, Wilbur, had died in 1912 from typhoid fever, but Orville was to see out the Second World War. Both would have been proud of the RB, whose

undercarriage was able to retract into wells in the fuselage to reduce drag – a revolutionary feature for the time. The high-mounted monoplane wing was of a cantilever type, and thus needed no bracing wires or struts, which again reduced drag, while the wing's leading and trailing edges could be raised or lowered to alter its curvature for extra control. To further reduce drag, there was no front glazing, the pilot having to

BELOW: René Arnoux's tailless Simplex racer of 1922.

OPPOSITE: The Thomas Morse TM22 racer, entered by the Army Air Service in the Pulitzer Trophy Race of 1922.

make do by looking out of small side windows. In the event, a problem with the wing's variable camber forced the innovative Dayton-Wright out of the

contest, although it certainly offered a foretaste of what was still to come.

During the 1920s and into the '30s, specialist racing aircraft followed a path of their own, leaving the modified warplanes behind. These became shorter and stubbier, and ever-larger and more powerful engines were shoehorned into streamlined noses. Similar in appearance, though designed not simply with speed in mind, was the Stipa monoplane (*page 79*). In the late 1920s, Luigi Stipa, of the Italian Air Ministry,

formulated the theory that mounting the engine and propeller inside a Venturi duct fuselage would increase thrust as the air accelerated down the narrower tube of the rear fuselage.

The prototype was a little over 19-ft (6-m) long, but it was nearly 11-ft (4-m) high, due to the large-diameter fuselage, which had to be that size to accommodate the 120-hp De Havilland Gipsy III engine. It looked extremely odd, but the Stipa flew suprisingly well, and its fat, stubby fuselage is said to

have contributed more than one-third of the required lift. The experiments continued, and ANF of France bought the rights to carry out its own tests, though nothing came of either development.

Returning to the pure racers, René Arnoux's Simplex of 1922 actually did without a tail, and raced at Étampes that year. A top speed of 236mph (380km/h) was claimed, using a 320-hp Hispano-Suiza, but the tailless Simplex was destroyed in a landing accident (the

OPPOSITE: The Granville brothers' Gee Bee Super-Sportster, competing in the Bendix Trophy race.

BELOW: Replica of the Gee Bee R-1.

pilot sustained only minor injuries) and never flew again.

Moving on a decade or so, and it becomes evident that tailfins hadn't disappeared after all. Typical of the 'all-engine' racers of the time was the Gee Bees series, built by the Granville brothers in the U.S.A. Their Super-Sportster, produced for the 1932 Thomson Trophy race, was only 17ft 9-in (5.4-m) long, with a 25-ft (8-m) wingspan, yet it packed a Pratt & Whitney Wasp engine of 800hp. These tiny planes seemed out of proportion, the huge engine cowling making up half the fuselage, surmounted by a tiny cockpit fairing and tail.

They may have looked odd but they were certainly fast, and the Super-Sportster won the Thomson Trophy that year, with James Doolittle piloting it to just over 252mph (405.5km/h). For the National Air

Races the following year, the same plane was uprated with a 900-hp supercharged Hornet engine; unfortunately, the pilot, Russell Boardman, was killed in the plane during the Bendix Trophy Race, and the Granville Aircraft Corporation closed down before the year was out.

But it was possible to fly fast on far less power, as the Crosby Special proved

in the 1936 National Air Races. It offered a mere 300hp from its six-cylinder in-line supercharged Menasco Buccaneer engine, but had a thin, pencil-like fuselage that was aerodynamically far more svelte than the short and stubby race planes. The pilot had to sit in a semi-reclined position, so thin was the stick-like fuselage. Designer Harry Crosby had reputedly been inspired by

BELOW: This replica of the 1931 Gee Bee Z appeared in the 1991 Walt Disney movie, The Rocketeer.

OPPOSITE: The Gee Bee R-2 Super-Sportster. The original 1932 R-2 was built for the Bendix Trophy Race (cross-country race), and was powered by the very same Pratt & Whitney R985 that had powered the 1931 Model Z, rated at 535hp.

the shape of a flying fish, and was doing well in the race when an oil-pipe broke, covering the windshield with lubricant and leaving him to settle for sixth place.

Although jet aircraft outran the piston-engined planes during the Second World War, propeller-driven racing had carried on, its own classes being quite distinct from the absolute speed records set by jets. As ever, racing is a dangerous business, but there are plenty of pilots and constructors willing to risk lives, and big investments, to win races and break speed records. Interestingly enough, many of the most competitive piston-engined racers today are highly-modified versions of Second World War fighters. This may sound absurd, like driving a vintage Bentley in modern Formula One racing, but there is a good reason for this. In many ways, the Spitfires, Lightnings, Mustangs and Hellcats were the cream of piston-engined aircraft development, certainly in terms of speed, so it makes sense to carry on using them. Of course, the modern racers have been highly modified, with performance far in advance of the wartime originals; nevertheless the link still exists.

But The U.S. company, Scaled Composites, reasoned that better results could be had by designing a propeller aircraft from scratch, using modern technology and materials. Not only that, but the designer, Burt Rutan, also wanted to prevent vintage fighter planes from being extensively modified and sometimes destroyed during modern racing. It was also his intention to set a new propeller-driven speed record, as well as win races. The Pond Racer PR-01 was unusual to say the least: it was built of the latest composite materials, with a twin-boom layout, the front of each boom housing an Electramotive VG-30 turbocharged engine of between 800 and 1000hp, each with a four-bladed propeller.

The wings were short and swept forward, and the single main tailfin was flanked by two small 'butterfly' fins at the tips of the tailplane to optimize pitch and yaw stability. The pilot sat in a separate central nacelle, with an integral escape system in case the worst happened. It first flew in 1991, and despite competing at Reno the following year, proved disappointing. The company had been unable to get its sophisticated electronics to work properly, and in this application the engines were unable to deliver their promised power. Despite its encouraging specification, the Pond Racer was simply too slow to win races or break records. It was entered for the 1993 Reno races, but was destroyed in an accident while in preparation for them.

But the important part of this chapter resides in the interwar years, when designers were seeking to produce highly-specialized planes for carrying people, goods, or weapons, or for launching in mid-air, or for flying faster than anything else. They added up to some incredible aircraft, but the Second World War would produce some even stranger designs.

The highly original PR-01 Pond Racer, produced by Scaled Composites.

CHAPTER THREE
STRANGE BEASTS OF WAR

German engineering, according to the well-worn cliché, is among the most thorough in the world, being of the highest quality and efficiency while possibly being neither wildly innovative nor over-imbued with lateral thinking. Yet Germany produced some of the most extraordinary aircraft ever seen during the Second World War, which included giant powered gliders, asymmetrical reconnaissance planes, pioneering rocket-powered fighters, a cheap-to-make Volksjäger ('People's

WEIRD AIRCRAFT

OPPOSITE ABOVE: The Focke-Wulf Fw 189 Uhu.

OPPOSITE BELOW: The Blohm und Voss Bv 141, the most asymmetrical aircraft ever built.

BELOW: The Dornier Do 335 Pfeil 'centreline-thrust' fighter-bomber.

Fighter') jet with a wooden frame, and so on, making the Allied aircraft – apart from the flying jeep – seem positively conservative by comparison.

Most aircraft, whatever their type, shape or size, are at least symmetrical, but the Blohm und Voss Bv 141 was anything but. In 1937, the German military issued a requirement for a short-range tactical reconnaissance aircraft to replace the Henschel Hs 126. It had to be a three-seater with outstanding all-round vision, have a single engine of around 850hp, and be capable of army co-operation should the need arise.

STRANGE BEASTS OF WAR

LEFT: The Saab 21 was a Swedish fighter-attack aircraft that first took to the air in 1943. It was described as a very efficient weapons platform, and was designed in a twin-boom pusher configuration, where the propeller is mounted in the rear of the fuselage, pushing the aircraft forward.

BELOW: The Convair R3Y Tradewind, a 1950s American turboprop-powered flying boat, designed and built by Convair.

OPPOSITE: The British Boulton Paul P.92, a large twin-engined three-seater long-range escort fighter, with an armament of four 20-mm cannon in a dorsal turret faired into the upper surface of the high wing.

It was a wide brief, and the three competing designs put forward to meet it were all quite different. By rights, the twin-boom Focke-Wulf Fw 189 Uhu should never have made it past the first hurdle, being twin-engined, yet it remained the military's favoured option, while the second option, the Arado Ar 198, was a modified monoplane with a glazed ventral section around the fixed undercarriage legs.

But the third was quite different, and on seeing the brief, Richard Vogt, of Hamburger Flugzeugbau, was able to start with a clean sheet of paper, coming up with the Bv 141. (It became the Bv 141 after Hamburger changed its name to Blohm und Voss.) The three-man crew sat in an almost all-glass cabin, mounted on the starboard side of a single boom, which held the engine at one end, the tail at the other. The port wing was longer than the starboard, which counteracted the displaced centre of gravity caused by having the weight of the cabin on one side. This mass also counteracted the torque of the propeller.

The aircraft's design prompted a mixed response from the Reichsluftfahrtministerium (RLM, the Air Ministry) and made no impact on their decision to build the Fw 189. But Blohm und Voss, not to be daunted, decided to fund a prototype itself, which flew for the first time in February 1938, as a result of which, albeit reluctantly, the Bv 141 was placed on the shortlist.

The original prototype was followed by three more, then by five pre-production planes known as the A-series. Another five, the B-series, were then produced, with new asymmetrical tailplanes. One of these, a Bv 141-V10, underwent service evaluation in Saxony in late 1941, and there were plans to form a single operational Bv 141 unit on the Eastern Front as soon as possible. That was abandoned the following year when problems with the aircraft persisted, and other delays meant that the final B-series plane was not delivered for trials until May 1943, by which time the Fw 189 had been working the skies over the Eastern Front for some time.

The same year that Richard Vogt had been dreaming up the Bv 141,

Claudius Dornier was taking out a patent on another radical aircraft. But like the Bv 141, the Dornier Do 335 Pfeil (*page 89*) only made it into limited production, arriving too late to affect the outcome of the war.

It was based on the principle of 'centreline-thrust', using both tractor (forward-facing) and pusher (rearward-

The Ryan FR Fireball was a composite propeller- and jet-powered aircraft designed for the U.S. Navy during the Second World War. The Fireball entered service before the end of the war, but did not see combat. The fastest Fireball was the XFR-4 (below), which had a Westinghouse J34 turbojet engine and was some 100mph (160km) faster than the FR-1.

facing) propellers in line with one another, each with their own engine. It wasn't a new idea, and had been used in Germany as early as 1917 in the form of the Siemens-Schuckert Dr I triplane fighter. Dornier's refinement, however, was to squeeze both engines into the fuselage, the forward one in the conventional position and the rearward engine right at the back of the fuselage, driving the pusher propeller. The great advantage of this arrangement, of course, was to the aerodynamics: with both bulky power units tucked away inside the aircraft's skin, the result was the most 'slippery' design possible for a twin-engined machine.

This had never been tried before, so Dornier first contracted the company of Schempp-Hirth to build an experimental plane with centreline thrust, this time with only one engine of 80hp driving the pusher propeller via a shaft. This Goppingen Go 9 flew successfully in 1940, encouraging Dornier to present plans to the RLM for a full-sized

The Messerschmitt Me 163B Komet was the only operational rocket-powered aircraft of the Second World War. The combination of spectacular performance and the danger of the highly explosive rocket fuels make it a fascinating piece of aviation history.

centreline-thrust fighter. As with the asymmetrical Bv 141, however, the RLM was not sufficiently impressed to take it further, and in any case preferred Dornier to concentrate on its existing bombers and flying boats.

93

The project may have died there had the RLM not issued a requirement for a single-seater intruder aircraft in 1942, capable of high speed and with the ability to carry bombs weighing 1,102lbs (500kg). Dornier dusted off his blueprints, detailing the centreline-thrust, and re-presented the idea as Project 231. This time it was accepted, although the brief was soon widened to make the plane suitable as a heavy fighter, a fighter-bomber, a two-seater night-fighter, and as a long-range reconnaissance plane.

Named the Do 335 Pfeil, the first prototype flew in October 1943. It was a sleek machine, with a long-nosed appearance that also led to it being called the 'Anteater'. The trials went well, with only minor longitudinal-

BELOW: The Caproni Campini CC2 (N-1), the world's first 'jet' plane, in the early 1940s flew from Milan to Rome at a speed of 310mph (500km/h).

OPPOSITE BELOW: The forward swept-wing Junkers Ju 287V1, the world's first heavy jet bomber. The nosewheel fairings were deleted before the first flight took place, exposing B-24 Liberator wheels.

stability problems, and the 335 proved very fast, the top speed of 474mph (763km/h) making it one of the fastest piston-engined aircraft ever built. To meet the wider brief, all sorts of variants were planned, with a second cockpit due to be added for a radar operator in the night fighter.

Do 335s went into operational evaluation in July 1944, but progress toward production was slow, due largely to the late delivery of major components, such as the 1800-hp Daimler-Benz DB 603 engines. Only 13 production machines had been completed when the factory was overrun

by the U.S. Army, although some say that another 70 were under construction. Had it arrived a year earlier, perhaps the Anteater might have made a greater contribution to Germany's defence, and it certainly had the potential for destroying bombers. One intriguing variant, for which time eventually ran out, was the 535, for which, incredibly, a rear jet engine and front piston engine was planned.

FAREWELL TO PROPS
Without the problems that had beset the Do 335 and Bv 141, Germany's jet-powered aircraft would undoubtedly

have made a far greater contribution to the country's defence if they had been developed a year or two earlier. As it was, the few units of Me 262s and 163 Komets that did make it into combat had to keep moving bases in the face of the Allied advance, and production was also badly disrupted during the last months of the Third Reich.

Jet fighters, like the Messerschmitt Me 262, are perhaps the best-known of these last-ditch German jets, but there was a bomber, too. The Arado Ar 234 Blitz had been designed back in 1941, but turbojet engines were hard to come by, as the Reich gave priority to jet fighters rather than bombers. The Blitz did not fly until June 1943, having been designed to fly high and fast, with a single pilot in a pressurized cabin and with the added bonus of an ejector seat – both very advanced features for the time. Trials went well, the first two Ar 234s being reconnaissance versions without the ejector and pressurized cabin, and flying operations were being undertaken from July 1944. The following December, production machines began bombing missions during the Ardennes offensive. Two hundred and fifty had been built, but in the confusion of those closing stages of

BELOW, OPPOSITE & PAGE 98: The Heinkel He 162 Salamander, Germany's wartime Volksjäger 'People's Fighter'.

the war, many of them never reached operational base.

Just as advanced, but for different reasons, was the Junkers Ju 287 bomber. The Luftwaffe wanted a replacement for the flawed Heinkel He 177, and Germany's aircraft manufacturers put forward all sorts of radical ideas. Horten and Junkers both proposed flying-wing designs, with six and four engines respectively, while Blohm und Voss favoured a W-platform wing. In the end, the Ju 287 was given the go-ahead, despite being a fairly radical solution. It used swept-forward wings, which had all the advantages of swept-back wings

while moving the worst-handling characteristics much higher up the speed range. Power came from four Jumo 004 turbojets, two wing-mounted and two located on the forward fuselage.

By now Germany was finding itself in an increasingly desperate situation, so a Ju 287 prototype was built using existing parts to save time, which included an He 177 fuselage, a Ju 388 tail, and even American B-24 Liberator nosewheels; in the event that the four Jumos would prove insufficient for a fully-laden take-off, it also had two wing-mounted Walter rocket packs, which could be jettisoned once their job was done.

This 'bitza' machine was fast, recording 400mph (645km/h) in one shallow dive, but as German forces retreated back to home territory, the overwhelming need was for fighters rather than bombers, and the Ju 287 programme was accordingly abandoned.

Incredibly it was revived in 1945, even as Germany was staring defeat in the face, and a six-engined prototype Ju 287V2 was under construction as Soviet forces were overrunning the Junkers factory; it was intended that it should use six BMW 003A-1 engines, two of them mounted in the nose, the estimated top speed being 537mph

(864km/h). As with so much other captured German engineering, this prototype was spirited back to the motherland, where it was flown by the Soviets with swept-back wings.

But what Germany urgently needed from late 1944 to early '45 was not bombers at all, but defensive fighters, able to wreak havoc on the waves of Allied bombers, which by day and night were destroying not only German industry but also many civilian lives. Priority was therefore given to the Messerschmitt Me 262 and tiny Me 163 Komet. The Komet was actually the first rocket interceptor to go into combat. There had been research into rocket planes in Germany since the

The Messerschmitt Me 163 Komet, despite being a revolutionary aircraft, and capable of performance that was unrivalled at the time, proved ineffective as a fighter and was able to destroy very few Allied aircraft during the Second World War.

1920s, and the Italians had successfully flown a two-seater jet in the 1930s, its Caproni machine having made the trip from Milan to Rome at an average of 310mph (500km/h) in 1938. But the Komet was still one of the earliest Second World War jets, tested first as a glider, and in the summer of 1941 at Peenemunde, with power.

From the start, it was phenomenally fast, and even with the initial Walter HWK R11-203b engine, with 1,653lb of thrust, could reach 550mph (885km/h). Operational Komets used a 3,750-lb (1700-kg) motor, run on a volatile combination of T-Stoff (hydrogen peroxide and water) and C-Stoff (hydrazine hydrate, methyl alcohol and water). Thus powered, a Komet was able to acclerate from 250 to 600mph (400–965km/h) in seconds, climb to its near 40,000-ft (12190-m) ceiling in three-and-a-half minutes, and approach the speed of sound in dives.

In fact, when Komets went into action from July 1944, their very speed proved to be a mixed blessing; they were able to approach the lumbering B-17s so fast that the pilot only had time for a three-second burst before they were past the bombers and away. Such tremendous speed, of course, used

OPPOSITE & RIGHT: The Bachem Ba 349 Natter (Viper), a semi-expendable, vertically-launched piloted missile, was one of the several desperate yet ingenious measures improvised by the Germans to defend their skies. Used in a similar way as unmanned surface-to-air missiles, after a vertical take-off, which eliminated the need for airfields, most of the flight was radio-controlled from the ground.

up a great deal of fuel, almost twice as much as the designers had forecast, and enough for only eight minutes of powered flight. The tactic was to get airborne as the enemy aircraft were almost overhead, climb above them, then shut off the engine for a fast glide attack, after which there might or might not be enough fuel to climb again for another three-second burst.

Komets were also tricky aircraft to fly; they were forced to take off into the wind, as the rudder was inoperative at low speeds, and landing on skids (the wheels were dropped after take-off) at 137mph (220km/h) took skill and nerve, coming from the knowledge that their volatile fuel load could very easily explode; in fact, there were some horrendous accidents. And finally, despite the Komet's superb

performance, they failed to pick off many bombers.

The volatile Komet, therefore, with its special fuel mix and tricky flying technique, was not the ideal machine for a nation in the process of industrial and military collapse. What was needed was an aircraft that was not only fast enough to outrun Allied fighters (which meant a jet) but also very simple to build and fly, something that could be put together quickly by semi-skilled labour. It must also be capable of being flown by the relatively inexperienced,

given that many experienced Luftwaffe pilots had already been lost on the Eastern Front. In September 1944, rival manufacturers were given only a week to submit their proposals. Heinkel had a headstart, basing what it called its Project 1073 on its planned Spatz lightweight fighter. Work proceeded at a furious pace, a mock-up was produced by 20 September, and the contract was awarded nine days later. The prototype He 162 Salamander (*see page 96 et seq.*), complete with a wooden frame, flew on 6 December.

BELOW: The Fieseler Fi 103, better known as the V-1 (Vergeltungswaffe 1) flying bomb, was the first guided missile, being the forerunner of today's cruise missile.

OPPOSITE ABOVE: The Junkers Ju 322 Mammut, a heavy transport glider resembling a giant flying wing. Only two prototypes were ever built.

OPPOSITE BELOW: The Yokosuka MXY-7 Ohka, a purpose-built rocket-powered kamikaze aircraft, used by Japan toward the end of the Second World War.

Unfortunately for Germany's defence, putting the Salamander into production didn't go quite as fast. The authorities wanted 50 planes in January 1945 and up to 1,000 a month from March onwards, which failed to happen as factories and airfields were overrun by the Allies. In the end, nearly 300 were built, but only 116 got as far as being operational units, and even if they did, rarely had enough fuel to fly. The Salamander, also known as the Volksjäger or 'People's Fighter', had indeed been easy to build, but it wasn't easy to fly, and like the Third Reich's other jets came too late to make any difference to the outcome of the war.

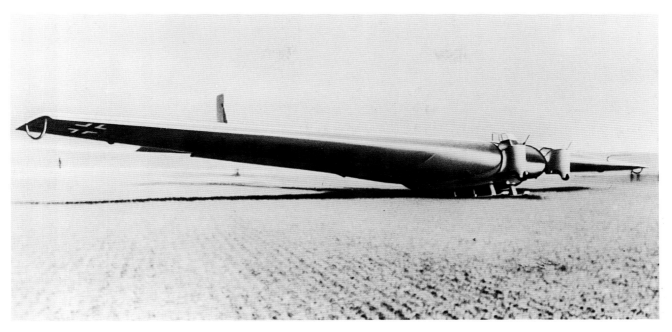

The Volksjäger was an advanced jet aircraft, but an aircraft nonetheless, designed to take off, perform its mission, and make it home.

Surface-to-air missiles, however, were a different matter, and Germany's V2 rocket was effective during the last months of the war. The Bachem Ba 349 Natter was interesting in that while part of it would be destroyed during a mission, part of it could be reused. It was powered by an Me 163 motor, here in its most thrusting form, with the addition of two or four solid-fuel

the pilot. The reality was that the Natter had only been test-launched 18 times, and only seven times with a pilot at the controls, so it was still very much in the development stage.

Better known is Germany's V1 flying bomb, but what is less well-

rocket boosters to help it blast off vertically from its launchpad. The aircraft took off and was guided almost to the bomber's altitude, using radio control from the ground, with the pilot taking control right at the end to point the nose in the right direction, jettison the plastic nosecone, and pull the trigger to fire off the 24 Hs 217 73-mm Föhn unguided rockets in one ferocious salvo. The pilot would then jettison the entire nosecone and cockpit and bale

out, when both he and the rear fuselage would hopefully be returned to base for the next mission.

In the event, no Natter got this far, as its development base at Kirkheim was captured by the Allies before it could enter combat. There had been successful test flights, but the first piloted launch in February 1945 ended badly when the Natter's canopy fell off, and after climbing to 5,000ft (1525m) the missile fell back to ground, killing

known is that there was a manned version, the Fieseler Fi 103R. It was intended to be air-launched from a bomber, then head for land and sea targets after the Allies invaded. In theory, the pilot had a chance of baling out just before impact, but in practice

the chances of surviving such a mission were small. This illustrates the small but significant cultural difference between the German approach to such missions and that of the Japanese: the Yokosuka MXY-7 Ohka, used from March 1945, was a rocket-powered

OPPOSITE: The Messerschmitt Me 323 Gigant powered glider transport.

BELOW: The Heinkel He 111Z Zwilling five-engined towing aircraft.

The Boeing YC-14 prototype, seen in flight in the mid 1970s, leading to both the AMST project and Light Weight Fighter.

suicide plane that allowed its pilot no means of escape.

Around 175 Fi 103Rs were actually built, but none of them saw service, the Luftwaffe having dropped the idea in favour of the Mistel composite aircraft. There was also the Me 328, built by Messerschmitt and powered by two Argus pulse jets, but which could also be air-launched from a glider. Carrying a 1,100- or 2,205-lb (500- or 1000-kg) bomb, this too was a non-reuseable aircraft, and again there was a nominal means of pilot escape.

INVASION GIANTS
Germany's jet aircraft will always be associated with the last desperate days of the war, but giant gliders had their heyday in 1940–41, when the war was going well for the Third Reich. Gliders had been used successfully to attack the Eben-Emael fort in Belgium in 1940, as well as for the invasion of Crete. In October of that year, Operation Sealion, the invasion of Britain, was postponed, the plan being to go ahead at a later date, and

Junkers and Messerschmitt were both asked to design giant gliders for the purpose. They would be larger than ever before, and be able to carry not only troops but also heavy armoured vehicles and even tanks.

As with so many wartime projects, this was urgent, and both companies were given only two weeks to come up with proposals. This they did, and the following month the RLM ordered 200 examples of both the Me 263 Gigant and Ju 322 Mammut.

To put it mildly, the Junkers Mammut (*page 103 above*) was not a success. The specification had been for an all-wooden glider – unlike the Gigant, with its tubular steel frame – and Junkers had little experience of using this material on such a scale. It decided on a flying-wing format, producing a massive span of 203ft 5in (62m) to accommodate the required load, though it also had a conventional boom-type fuselage to carry the tail. Cargo was stored in the deep centre section of the wing, accessed via detachable panels on the leading edge.

So far so good, except that in practice the wooden structure was seriously overweight, reducing the projected payload by 20 per cent. When

the test loading of a tank was attempted, it crushed the floor, which necessitated strengthening it to such a degree as to reduce the payload by another 22 per cent. The first flights caused more headaches in April 1941. The Ju 90 towing aircraft had to struggle to haul the heavy glider into the air, and when the Mammut's undercarriage was jettisoned, it hit the ground with such force that fragments rebounded back into the aircraft. Then the glider began to climb far too quickly, gaining height on the Ju 90 until it was pulling its tail up, which prevented it from climbing at all.

Fortunately, the Mammut's pilot realized the dangerous situation that was developing and released the towline, after which his craft became stabilized and was able to glide to a landing on its skid. Unfortunately, this was some way off from the airfield, and the Mammut was simply too big to be hoisted onto the back of a truck and driven back the same day. In fact, it took two weeks for it to be towed very slowly by tanks.

Junkers began the inevitable redesign, but in May the project was cancelled. However, because of the perceived urgency of the situation, 98

Mammuts had already been built which would never be used, thus creating a huge waste of resources for Germany's increasingly beleaguered war economy. But they weren't completely wasted: all 98 wooden gliders were eventually chopped up for firewood.

Messerschmitt's Gigant (*page 104*) was rather more successful. This, too, as the name suggests, was a huge aircraft, with a wingspan of 181ft 3in (55m) and a 35-tonne laden weight, although it could be overloaded up to nearly 40 tonnes. The load space was 36-ft long, 11-ft high and 10-ft wide (11 x 3.3 x 3m), accessed through large clamshell doors in the nose, and big enough to swallow 200 troops. Flight trials began in February 1941, a couple of months before the Mammut, and once again the Ju 90 towplane struggled to do its job. The good news was that the Gigant was stable and flew well, once it was airborne, and it was used for logistics support on the Eastern Front.

OPPOSITE: The Westland P.12 Lysander was intended to repel a German invasion of Britain by strafing beaches and striking at surface vessels, or for use as a trainer for RAF gunners.

But the problem with the biggest operational glider of the Second World War was still how to get it into the air. The Ju 90 was clearly not up to the task, and the immediate solution was to tow it using three Messerschmitt Bf 110 fighters in triangular formation. It worked, after a fashion, but was a hazardous undertaking, and one accident saw all three 110s lost, plus the glider and its load of 120 troops. It was so dangerous that the triple 110 set-up had to be restricted on the snow-covered Eastern Front, if not postponed altogether, although by then there was an operational unit made up of 18 gliders and 36 Bf 110s.

The solution was the Heinkel He 111Z Zwilling (*page 105*), one of the strangest-looking aircraft to see service in the war. If the Zwilling looked like two He 111H bombers welded together,

BELOW: The Chance Vought V-173 small-scale Skimmer demonstrator.

OPPOSITE ABOVE & BELOW: The Curtiss XP-55 Ascender. It achieved 390mph (628km/h), but never saw production.

it is because it was, or at least it was something very similar. The two bombers were joined at the wings, like

Siamese twins, with a fifth engine
mounted between the two cockpits. The
Zwilling was available from the middle
of 1942 and proved up to the job of
towing a 35-tonne Gigant into the air.
The plan was to use Zwilling-towed
Gigants for the invasion of Malta,
which in the event was cancelled; they
might even have played a part in
resupplying German forces at
Stalingrad, but did not become
available until it was too late.

Special towing aircraft, underwing rockets to help take-off – these things were tried, but the ultimate solution was perhaps the most obvious, to give the Gigant some permanent power of its own. This was the Me 323, basically a Gigant glider fitted with six Gnôme-Rhône 14N 48/49 radial engines of 1140hp each. Early prototypes had used four engines, but six provided a safety margin. Flight trials began in spring 1942, with the first production Me 323s going into service late that year.

The Gigant was instantly transformed from a glider, that would possibly be utilized only once, into a reuseable transport plane. The Me 323 had permanent landing gear, tough enough for it to cope with bumpy fields, so it was quite flexible as to where it could operate. One of its first jobs was to support the Afrika Korps, and much later many were used to evacuate troops from the collapsing Eastern Front. But the Gigant-with-engines was not a

BELOW: A Vultee XP-54 pressurized fighter.

OPPOSITE: The North American P-82 (F-82) Twin Mustang was the last American piston-engined fighter ordered into production by the U.S. Air Force.

The Vought F7U Cutlass, a highly unusual, semi-tailless design, was a U.S. Navy carrier-based jet fighter and fighter-bomber of the early Cold War era.

perfect war machine. It lumbered along at only 130mph (210km/h) or so, despite its prodigious power, making it an easy target for enemy fighters; but its tubular steel, wood and fabric structure proved surprisingly tough, enabling it to absorb a good deal of punishment, although the extra weight of the engines and landing-gear meant that the payload was drastically reduced to 10–12 tonnes. By 1944, however, Germany was facing the kind of war that was very different from the one in which the giant gliders had been conceived; it was now on the defensive rather than the offensive.

ALLIED AERONAUTICS AND FLYING JEEPS

German aircraft manufacturers had been able to come up with many radical ideas to aid the war effort, but the Allies also had some unusual concepts of their

own. While Britain was waiting for an imminent German invasion, thoughts were turning to how best forces landing on England's beaches could be attacked. The Westland P12 (*page 108*) was one suggestion, being a variation on the company's Lysander army co-operation machine. The rear fuselage was truncated and was fitted with a tail-gun turret, plus a rear-mounted 'tandem wing' with end-plate fins and rudders to compensate for any lack in longitudinal

stability over the longer Lysander. The P12 was thought to be just the thing to strafe invasion troops paddling ashore, or surface vessels sitting not far off the coast. It first flew in July 1941 and was found to be highly manoeuvrable. But as the threat of invasion began to fade, so too did the need for this highly specialized aircraft, and it never reached production.

While the P12 looked distinctly odd, the Chance Vought F5U Skimmer,

by contrast, didn't look at all unusual, although its design brief was very strange. It was intended to be a naval fighter that could fly at extremely low speeds, even at a slow hover, and at up

The Sud-Ouest SO 6020 Espadon was an experimental interceptor, with slightly swept wings and a jet engine in the tail with a ventral intake. The aircraft was underpowered, and many experiments followed in an effort to cure this fault.

to 425mph (685km/h). Two Pratt & Whitney R-2000 Twin Wasp piston engines provided the power, at 1350hp, but the Skimmer's secret weapon was its propellers, which had four articulated blades that could act like helicopter rotors when the aircraft was at a high angle of attack. The crew sat in a glazed cockpit in front of the near-circular wing/fuselage, and armour was to be four 20-mm cannon and two 0.50-in (1.27-mm) machine guns. The Skimmer would also, according to the plan, carry two 1,000-lb (454-kg) bombs.

To test the concept, as Dornier had with the centreline-thrust Do 335, first a smaller-scale prototype was built. This was the V-173 (*page 110*), with a wood-and-fabric structure and power from two 80-hp Continental C80 engines. It made a successful test flight in November 1942, but development appears to have proceeded at a slow pace, for it was some time before two full-sized Skimmer prototypes were ordered and the first wasn't completed for testing until well after the end of the war: it never flew.

The Sud-Est SE 5000 (5003) Baroudeur was a light, simple jet fighter without undercarriage. Take-off was by a rocket-powered trolley, and it landed on skis on a grass strip, the advantages being simplicity and independence from airfields. The disadvantage of such an arrangement was the difficulty in the handling of landed aircraft.

WEIRD AIRCRAFT

Although the Allies, and particularly the British, were pioneering jet aircraft, they also persevered with piston-engined prototypes, while the U.S.A.F. experimented with pusher propellers in several forms. One was the Curtiss XP-55 Ascender (*page 111*), powered by a single Allison V-1710 engine of 1275hp in the rear fuselage, driving a three-blade pusher propeller. It had rear-mounted swept-back wings and winglets, and small canards, with armament consisting of two 20-mm cannon and four 0.50-inch machine guns. Three prototype Ascenders were built, and the first flew in July 1943, attaining 390mph (628km/h) while never reaching production.

The Vultee XP-54 (*page 112*) was another pusher-propeller aircraft, using contra-rotating blades powered by a 2300-hp Lycoming XH-2470-1 unit. It had a pressurized cockpit and cranked wings, and two prototypes were built, the first flying in January

The Sud-Ouest SO 9000 (9050) Trident had a small straight wing, with jet engines fitted to the wingtips and a rocket engine in the tail. It was intended as an interceptor, with one very large AAM under the fuselage. The Trident had exceptional performance, but the SO 9050 Trident II (below) was redesigned to cure some of Trident I's faults, and after two prototypes of the latter, six pre-production aircraft were ordered. The programme, however, was cancelled in 1958.

The Rotabuggy (formally known as the Malcolm Rotaplane) was an experimental aircraft that was essentially a Willys MB jeep combined with an autogyro.

1943, but like the Ascender, failed to proceed further. The XP-56 was yet another pusher prototype, built by Northrop and developed a few months later than the Vultee. It, too, used contra-rotating pusher propellers, though with slightly less power from its 2000-hp Pratt & Whitney unit. Perhaps the XP-56's main innovation was its wings, which had anhedral outer panels, and the tail, which comprised only dorsal and ventral fins, while spoilers on the upper and lower surfaces of the anhedral panels, and elevators on the wing trailing-edges, provided control.

Remember the Zwilling, that used two Heinkel bombers to build a towplane strong enough to haul a giant glider into the air? The U.S.A.F. had a different role in mind for the P-82 Twin Mustang (*page 113*), consisting of two P-51 Mustang fighters, complete with twin-piloted cockpits. Designed toward the end of the Second World War, it was intended for long-range escort and night-fighter duties in the Pacific. Two hundred and seventy were built, one of which achieved the first American air victory of the Korean War, when it shot down a Yakovlev Yak-9.

Jets, hovering fighters, giant gliders, all of them were incredible in their own way, but perhaps none was quite as weird as the flying jeep. This was a British idea, developed from the Rotachute, being basically a seat with two rotor blades on top, which could make a controlled descent from an air launch and had enough lift to carry a man and a Bren gun. Much went into the project, and the Rotachute certainly worked, although the wartime circumstances to suit it never arrived.

However its designer, Raoul Hafner, was not to be deterred. He had designed a helicopter as early as 1929 in Austria, but by 1941 was helping the war effort in England, working at the Airborne Forces Experimental Establishment in Manchester. Why not think bigger, he reasoned, and apply the same principles of the Rotachute to larger

loads, as a Rotabuggy, or even a Rotatank, based on a Valentine tank.

History does not record whether the Rotatank ever worked, but a contract to develop the Rotabuggy, based on a U.S. Army jeep, was awarded to the ML Aviation Company in 1942. The initial tests involved loading a jeep with concrete and dropping it from heights of up to 7ft 8in (2.3m), proving that the tough little four-wheel-drive could cope with strong impacts and drive away unscathed. So the hapless vehicle was fitted with a 46ft 8-in (14-m) two-blade rotor, controlled via a 'hanging' lever next to the steering wheel, and a streamlined tail fairing with twin rudderless fins; since the Rotabuggy was expected to glide, glider navigational instruments were also installed.

The next step was a tow test, and in November 1943, fastened to the back of a four-litre supercharged Bentley, the flying jeep did indeed fly, or at least glide, at up to 65mph (105km/h). Later flights were made using a Whitley bomber as the towing vehicle, which proved a little disconcerting for the pilot/driver in the jeep. A witness described how she watched the Whitley take off with the jeep in tow, circle, and

then land. Unfortunately, the jeep failed to touch down at the same time, but made a series of up-and-down movements instead. The witness judged the occupants to be 'unhappy', which must have been something of an understatement, with one clutching the rotor control and the other the steering wheel. Eventually, the jeep was able to stay down, but being still attached to the Whitley, the driver was forced to go flat-out to keep up.

When it stopped, the driver and pilot did not get out. They were helped out by onlookers, who found that the pilot was exhausted, presumably not only from terror but also from the effort of holding onto the joystick, which had been whipped into circles during the whole flight. According to official records, most of the Rotabuggy's flights were more successful than this, and it was classed as 'highly satisfactory' overall, especially after larger tailfins and greater rotor-blade articulation were added.

So the Rotabuggy may well have gone to war, had the development of the Horsa and Hamilcar vehicle-carrying gliders made it unnecessary. Doubtless, one or two test pilot/drivers would have been mightily relieved!

CHAPTER FOUR

FLYING WINGS

Surely all aircraft need tails and conventional fuselages, don't they? Not according to countless inventors and corporations, which have sought to perfect the 'flying wing' for more than 100 years. Yet these have only relatively recently made the leap from being one-off prototypes to full production aircraft, albeit as limited and highly specialized machines.

Back in 1876, a young Frenchman, Alphonse Pénaud, was convinced he had the answer, and filed a patent for an amphibious machine that consisted of a one-piece monoplane wing. In fact, it was packed with radical ideas, some of which would not make it onto a working aircraft for 500 years. The Pénaud wing featured variable-pitch propellers, a glazed cockpit, and retractable undercarriage. Predictably it

was met with ridicule, and its inventor, discouraged and depressed, committed suicide in 1880 when he was only 30 years old.

Pénaud's wing, of course, never got further than the drawing board,

OPPOSITE: The Dunne D.4. Note the erratic white lines painted on the wings and fins, which were intended to disguise the aircraft's unique shape.

ABOVE: The tailless Dunne Biplane.

but fast forward 30 years or so to when Lieutenant John Dunne was working on a full-sized flying wing, which would eventually see success. Dunne designed kites, big enough to carry a single man, for the British Army's Balloon Factory at Farnborough, while in his spare time he was working on what he hoped would be an inherently stable flying machine. He decided to build a glider in 1905, intending to fit an engine to it for later trials.

His employers were so taken with the idea that it was officially adopted. The first Dunne glider was therefore financed by the government and was built from the start, under a cloak of secrecy, as a military project. The D.1 was a biplane, its two wings aligned in a V-shape, carefully designed to provide maximum stability. It crashed after a short flight, but the results were adequately encouraging for two engines to be fitted. Unfortunately, they were puny 7.5-hp units, insufficient to power

the D.1 into the sky, even with the help of a downward ramp.

By 1908 the D.1 had been damaged and repaired; it was renamed the D.4 and was fitted with wingtip fins, a pilot's nacelle, and fixed undercarriage. There was even a new 25-hp engine but this, too, proved unequal to the task, enabling the D.4 to achieve nothing more than brief hops.

By this time, Dunne's paymasters had lost patience and had withdrawn funding, but the man himself was convinced of his plane's potential; he left Farnborough, taking D.4 with him. He was able to find backing elsewhere, and the Marquis of Tullibardine, on whose land the original trials had taken place, funded a D.5 to be built by Short Brothers, this time with a 60-hp engine driving twin pusher propellers

This was rather more successful: not only was the D.5 able to fly, which it first did in 1910, but like the very first prototype it also proved to be extremely stable. On one occasion, Dunne amazed a crowd of onlookers, which included Orville Wright, by sitting in the D.5 without touching the controls as it flew itself in a steady, straight line. In the process he only narrowly missed a windmill, but the

The Burgess-Dunne seaplane of 1914.

point had been made. It was made even more graphically by a French pilot in the D.5's successor, the D.8, when, leaving the controls, Dunne walked out onto the wing, then back again, as the D.8 flew itself. It was a testament to the fundamental stability of the flying-wing design, though for military pilots it would prove just a little too stable, in that it lacked the tight-turning manoeuvrability desirable in a good fighter.

GLIDERS & JETS

But in the 1920s, that was yet to be recognized, as Captain G.T.R. Hill designed the Pterodactyl, a tailless machine so stable that it could be manoeuvred in a stall. The design was adopted by Westland Aircraft, and as with Dunne's D.1, initial tests were of a glider before the first powered version flew in 1926. It showed so much promise that the Air Ministry took over the project, spawning a whole line of variations on the theme, including the 80-hp Mk 1B and the Mk IV, a three-seater with an enclosed cabin. In the early 1930s, Westland built the Mk V sesquiplane, a two-seater fighter powered by a 600-hp Rolls-Royce Goshawk engine.

In Germany, too, development of flying wings was on the move, although 14 years of work produced what were mostly prototypes. Reimar and Walter Horten built their Ho I glider in 1931, with the pilot lying prone to accommodate the aerodynamic wing profile. It wasn't a great success, but the modified Ho II fared rather better; four prototypes were built, one of which was fitted with an 80-hp Hirth engine,

enabling it to make its first powered flight in 1935, the remaining Ho Is all being gliders.

A whole succession of gliders followed through the late 1930s, until the two-seater Ho V took off in 1938, powered by two Hirth units. A Ho VII trainer followed, powered by two Argus 240-hp units. During the Second World War, the Ho flying wings became part of the Luftwaffe's jet programme, with the Ho IX planned as a single-seater jet-powered fighter, with two BMW 109-003A-1 engines. This it would have been

BELOW: The Westland-Hill Pterodactyl Mk 1B.

OPPOSITE: The Horten Ho IX V1, planned to take two BMW turbojets, was finally tested as a glider in 1944.

but for a miscalculation: when the engines arrived, they were found to be too big to fit between the spars of the Ho IX, which was finally tested as a glider in 1944.

Meanwhile, a redesigned V2 version was built around two Junkers

109-004B-1 turbojets. This was rather more successful, first flying in early 1945 and achieving nearly 500mph (805km/h), though not for long; the V2 crashed after a total of only two hours' flying time. By this time, the entire programme had been transferred to Gotha, under which the German flying wings came much closer to production. Seven prototypes and 20 pre-production planes were built, all developments of the V2. A V3 fighter-bomber prototype was also designed,

equipped with four 30-mm cannon and two 2,204-lb (1000-kg) bombs; they were almost ready for flight-testing when the factory was overrun by the U.S. Army.

Other variants were in the pipeline for the Go 229A project, as the Ho had been renamed, including a V7 tandem two-seater trainer and a V4 day and night fighter. These failed to get to the flying prototype stage, but it was estimated that the Go 229A had the potential for achieving 607mph

(977km/h) maximum. Nor were there only military variants on the drawing board. The Ho VIII was intended to be an airliner with a 157-ft (48-m) wingspan, big enough to seat 60 passengers and powered by six 600-hp BMW piston engines driving pusher propellers. A prototype was initiated, and if the Ho VIII had been brought to fruition it would probably have been converted as a bomber.

Much later the Ho VIII resurfaced in Argentina as the I.A.38 cargo plane, now with a wingspan of 105ft (32m) and a fuselage nacelle big enough to swallow six tonnes of cargo. Why Argentina? Well Reimer Horten, co-originator of the entire series, had emigrated there in 1948, after Germany was prohibited from developing further aircraft. His designs relied on wooden airframes, and his preferred spruce and birchwood simply weren't available, while the local glue was of an inferior quality. Despite the difficulties, he did manage to build several gliders, and the I.Ae 38 first flew in December 1960, powered by four 450-hp I.a.16E1 Gaucho piston engines, even though it was eventually cancelled altogether.

In the best traditions of Dunne and Hill, British interest in the concept of the tailless aircraft persisted throughout the Second World War, and was evident in the designs of Handley Page, Armstrong Whitworth, General Aircraft Ltd., and De Havilland. A rather undistinguished model of the period, with a decidedly chequered

The Armstrong Whitworth A.W.52 was a British flying-wing aircraft design of the late 1940s.

ABOVE & PAGE 128: The Fieseler F3 Lippisch Delta IV, a sport monoplane with folding wings. The plane was intended as an entry in the European Rally, taking place in 1932, but the resultant aircraft was too hastily designed and failed to fulfil what was required of it.

service life, was the Handley Page Manx, delivered in 1939 and so-called because of its vestigial tail. Designed by Dr. Gustav Lachman, the Manx used two in-line pusher engines, with wingtip vertical fins and rudders, slats, elevons, and split flaps for control. The Manx seemed promising, but its trials proved inauspicious; the prototype was

found to be 3,300lb (1497kg) overweight, and the main spar joints had to be reworked because of glue deterioration. Taxi tests began in February 1940, but there were many interruptions and the aircraft proved reluctant to fly, though it did reach an altitude of 12ft (3.6m) after hitting a bump in the runway. It actually flew in

June 1943, but the flight was aborted after only ten minutes when it was evident that the canopy had been lost. When the project was abandoned in 1946, the Manx had amassed only 17 hours flying time over 30 flights.

At the same time, General Aircraft Limited was experimenting with flying-wing gliders with different degrees of backward sweep. Four were built, of which the GAL 56/03 Maximum V was typical, in that it had a 36.4-degree sweep-back and nose flaps. It also had two sets of split flaps, one hinged at the 50 per cent chord line, one at the 70 per cent line, though only one set could be used at a time, with the changeover taking place on the ground.

It seemed like an ideal testbed for the whole concept, but Captain Eric M. Brown R.N. (retired), former chief naval test pilot at the Royal Aircraft Establishment, Farnborough, was less than impressed. 'It was one plane in which I found I could not relax for a second,' he later recalled, 'beginning right away with take-off. I could not lift it off the ground through the slipstream of the towing aircraft before the latter was airborne, which was the normal method, because as soon as it was clear of the ground effect cushion of air,

between wingtip and ground, the centre of pressure suddenly shifted and the machine dived straight back into the ground, to bounce on its very springy undercarriage wildly across the airstrip… The stalling characteristics also made landing very tricky.'

Meanwhile, G.T.R. Hill, the designer of the Pterodactyl, was having more luck in Canada, having designed an experimental glider for the National Research Council. This was relatively conventional, with the usual elevons, fins and rudders at the wingtips, plus

retractable landing gear. The prototype revealed good flight characteristics and flew some 105 hours, including the time taken to tow it 2,300 miles (3700km) across Canada.

The Handley Page H.P. 75 Manx.

Back in Britain, the respected firm of Armstrong Whitworth had had a post-war vision of a flying-wing airliner, and actually began work on the project during the war. The development process was slow and methodical, starting with wind-tunnel tests on models, then on the A.W. 52G half-scale glider, on which work had begun in May 1942, though the demands of war work meant that it wasn't towed for flight-testing until three years later. It was intended to combine the advantages of a tailless design with those of a laminar-flow wing. Armstrong Whitworth's team calculated that such an aircraft would have a total parasitic drag about one-third of that of a conventional machine. The ultimate goal was a passenger-carrying airliner weighing up to 200,000lbs (90720kg).

The initial flight tests went well enough to proceed with two powered versions, the first with two 5,000-lb thrust Rolls-Royce Nene turbojets, mounted in the centre section of the wing each side of the cockpit. It was designed for speeds of 400–500mph (645–800km/h), had an ejector seat, a pressurized cockpit, retractable landing gear, and thermal de-icing of the wings using exhaust heat. It was first flown in November 1947, with a second prototype, with Rolls-Royce Derwents, following a year or so later. Sadly the results were disappointing: the wings did not have laminar flow, and the A.W. 52 (*page 126*) proved very sensitive to elevator control, needing longer take-off and landing distances than a comparable conventional aircraft. The first prototype was lost in May 1949, due to an asymmetrical

flutter that prompted the pilot to abandon the plane. The second was used for more research into airflow behaviour over swept-back wings until it was finally dropped in September 1953.

NORTHROP FORGES AHEAD

The most successful and far-reaching flying-wing research, that eventually led to a limited production aircraft, did not come out of Europe at all but from the United States, where Northrop was the leading protagonist, having worked on

OPPOSITE: General Aircraft Ltd.'s GAL 56 Maximum V was a British tailless swept-wing glider design of the 1940s

BELOW: The GAL 56 Medium U, with parallel-chord centre section,

such craft in the 1930s. Its first flyer was the N-1M in 1940, a relatively small twin-engined machine with a wingspan of 38ft (11.6m), whose job it was to prove that the theory worked before Northrop began building a large twin-engined flying-wing cargo. With two

BELOW RIGHT: British inventiveness stimulated an inflatable-wing aircraft, produced by ML Aviation Ltd. as the Utility in the mid-1950s. Twelve wings were tested and three aircraft were built, XK776, XK781 and XK784.

OPPOSITE: The first of the Northrop flying-wing bombers. The B-35 Flying Wing was designed as an intercontinental bomber, competing with the B-36. It was powered by four large radial engines installed within the wing.

65-hp piston engines (120-hp units were fitted later), the N-1M demonstrator (*page 135*) was highly successful, making over 200 flights, and was certainly a more competent aircraft than any other flying-wing prototype up until that time.

Northrop's original plan for a peacetime flying wing was soon overtaken by the demands of war, and in 1942 work began on a bomber. As with the earlier project, a smaller-scale version was built to prove the technology. In fact, there were four of them, all with 60-ft (18-m) wingspans and twin engines, and bearing the tag N-9M (*page 134*). Like the N-1M, these proved highly successful and performed their job well.

The full-sized plane, the XB-35, was finally completed in 1946, and in classic flying-wing style, the 172-ft (52-m) wingspan formed the aircraft's main structure, with an offset cockpit for the single pilot. The XB-35 was full-sized in every respect, and dwarfed the wartime B-17 Flying Fortress, having almost three times the wing area and gross weight, its take-off weight being nearly 95 tonnes, with a payload of over 33 tonnes. Five other crew sat in the wing's centre section, with a rear gunner in a tail blister that had four remote-control two-gun turrets. Power came from four 3000-hp Pratt & Whitney R-4360 Wasp Major piston engines. Big piston aircraft were then near the end of their development before turbojets took over, but these were state of the art, having

turbo-superchargers and driving contra-rotating pusher propellers.

The YB-35 made its first flight in June 1946, soon followed by a second prototype with single, rather than contra-rotating, propellers. Both evidently showed promise, for eight more prototypes were ordered, plus five YB-35A pre-production machines. But the piston engines were fast becoming outdated, and two of these YB-35s were converted into jet bombers as YB-49s. The YB was a large aircraft, but the jet engines also made it fast, with eight 4,000-lb (1815-kg) Allison J-35-A-5

turbojets boosting the top speed to 520mph (837km/h). Intake air came via the leading-edge of the wings, with dorsal and ventral fins added each side of the engine groups. A variation on the theme was the YRB-49 reconnaissance bomber, using four 5,600-lb (2540-kg) J-35-A-21 turbojets in the wing trailing-edges and two more in underwing pods. Yet despite extensive research work, the YBs never made it into full production: orders were received for 30 YB-49s and 200 X-35s, but both were cancelled.

Not only were there bombers, but there was also a Northrop flying-wing fighter as well. The company had created America's first jet-powered military plane in 1944, by fitting an Aerojet XCAL-200 motor to its MX-234 glider. That led to the XP-79B, still a flying wing but with two 1,150-lb (522-kg) Westinghouse 19B turbojets and a wingspan of 38ft (11.6m). Armed with four 0.50-inch machine guns, the XP-79B could reach 510mph (821km/h). However, its real

innovation lay in the wings, the clue being in its nickname of the Flying Ram. The wings were made of welded magnesium plate, strong

OPPOSITE: The Northrop N-9M was a one third-scale model of the larger flying-wing B-35s and YB-49s.

ABOVE: The Northrop N-1M technology demonstrator, with original anhedral wingtips and two 65- or (later) 120-hp piston engines.

enough to slice through the tails of enemy bombers.

A ramming plane that could slice its enemy to ribbons and fly away unscathed sounds like the stuff of science fiction, but that was a serious intent behind this extraordinary aircraft. The pilot lay in a prone position, partly to enhance the aerodynamics, there being no need of a bubble cockpit to spoil the smooth lines, and partly to protect him from the airborne debris resulting from a mid-air ramming mission. Perhaps it was fortunate that the Flying Ram never got as far as ramming anything, for 15 minutes into its first flight, in September 1945, the plane went out of control and was destroyed.

By then, of course, the war was over, and no doubt Northrop had its eye on the civilian potential of a flying wing. An airliner version of the YB-49 was planned, with 48 seats on the main deck and an upper deck lounge in place of the bomber's fire-control blister. It would have made a fast long-distance people-carrier, with a range of 2,258 miles (3634km) at an average 511mph (822km/h), or nearly 3,500 miles (5633km) if the pilot throttled back to 382mph (615km/h). But like

The Northrop XP-79B Flying Ram was an ambitious American design for a flying-wing fighter aircraft, in that it had several notable design features, one of them being that the pilot operated the aircraft from a prone position. It also had a welded magnesium monocoque structure rather than the more usual one of riveted aluminium.

the bomber, it never reached production, and the hoped-for mass orders never materialized.

But it was not the end of Northrop's involvement with flying wings, and the most spectacular part of the story was still to come. This was the 'stealth bomber', now one of the most famous aircraft in the world and the point at which the flying-wing concept, after nearly a century of experimentation, finally made it into operational use. What made this possible was computer control. By the 1970s, aircraft designers were developing fighters like the F-16 that were very unstable in flight, and thus highly manoeuvrable, but which were made controllable by means of sophisticated electronics. Exactly the same technology could make a large flying wing both manoeuvrable and

stable, which is why it was announced in 1978 that the U.S.A.F. was to have an all-new bomber for strategic missions over enemy territories. Northrop duly submitted its flying wing for the 21st century, and the contract was awarded in 1981.

Eight years later, the Northrop-Grumman B-2 Spirit, to use its full official title, was rolled out onto the tarmac of Air Force Plant 42, Palmdale, California. It made its first flight in July 1989, making the journey to Edwards Airforce Base for further tests. This was the first of six development B-2s, though in all there would be 21 in operational work. But that was 15 years away, due to numerous developmental problems and the sheer complexity of delivering such a sophisticated machine.

But what was so special about the stealth bomber? By modern jet fighter-bomber standards it wasn't particularly fast (it could cruise at Mach 0.8) and the idea of the flying wing was nothing new. The clue lay in the word 'stealth'. The B-2 was designed to fly far and high over enemy territory, and it positively bristled with technology that allowed it to do this without it being spotted.

LEFT & PAGES 140 & 141: The Northrop-Grumman B-2 Spirit, a multi-role stealth heavy bomber, capable of deploying both conventional and nuclear weapons. Its development was a milestone in the modernization programme of the U.S. Department of Defense, and it is operated exclusively by the U.S. Air Force. The B-2's stealth technology was intended to aid the aircraft's penetration role, in order that it would survive extremely dense anti-aircraft defences otherwise considered impenetrable by combat aircraft.

The contrails, normally a giveaway in jets, were reduced by managing the temperature of the exhaust gas, and there was 'low-probability-of-intercept' strike radar, with emitters that could be turned off when the aircraft went into attack mode. Fending off radar was central to the entire stealth concept, so the B-2 was built of composites, with special finishes to reduce its infra-red 'signature'; so also was the honeycomb internal structure, the idea being to absorb and dissipate radar energy rather than deflect it straight back to the ground station. In flight, with the land gear up, the B-2 resembled a menacing stingray, being devoid of vertical stabilizers or control surfaces.

Instead, a series of elevons and split surfaces acted as ailerons, elevators, airbrakes, rudders and flaps.

Despite its slim profile, the B-2 could carry as many bombs as the larger, conventional B-52, though all of these were carried internally to keep the shape aerodynamically 'clean'. Two bays in the centre fuselage held up to 40,000lb (18145kg) of weaponry, and with such a large payload, and all the technology on board, the B-2 ended up as a large, heavy aircraft, with a wingspan of 172ft (52m) and a take-off weight of over 156 tonnes. With 14.5 tonnes of bombs on board, it could fly 6,900 miles (11105km), or over 11,500 miles (18507km) if in-flight refuelling was utilized.

The original plan was to build 133 operational stealth bombers, but with a price-tag of over $2 billion apiece, this ambition was soon curtailed and only 21 were in service by 1997. Even now, much of the B-2's detailed specification is shrouded in mystery, as are many of its missions, though it did play a major role in the bombing of the former Yugoslavia in 1999. The B-2 was certainly effective, and was a huge technological achievement, although the ethics of spending $2 billion on a

single aircraft have been questioned, when such a sum could have transformed the lives of thousands living on the ground. But that, of course, has long been a discussion-point whenever the subject of expensive weaponry is raised.

In some ways, the B-2 represented the application of new technology to older ideas. The flying wing was neither new nor, since the advent of radar, is stealth technology. Lockheed had been one of the specialists in avoiding radar, pioneering the field at its 'Skunk Works' and applying this research to existing U.S.A.F. planes in the 1960s.

Many of these ideas were incorporated into the SR-71 Mach 3 strategic reconnaissance aircraft that first appeared in 1964, and there was a YF-12 interceptor version as well, which never got beyond the prototype stage.

The Skunk Works' research culminated in Lockheed's F-117A Nighthawk stealth fighter, the first operational plane to fully exploit these advanced anti-radar features and which, in fact, went far beyond deflecting radar. Entering service with the U.S.A.F. in August 1982, the Nighthawk sought to keep a low profile through minimizing anything that

might advertise its presence, including noise and electromagnetic emissions, contrails, engine-exhaust smoke, infra-red, its visual profile and, of course, radar.

The skin of the aircraft consisted of many angled plates that would deflect an incoming radar beam away, rather than straight back to its source. All aircraft produce heat, and infra-red heat-seeking missiles are designed to exploit the fact, but the Nighthawk reduced the risk of being noticed with the use of non-afterburning engines, and by the cooling of the exhaust smoke, while shielded exhaust nozzles,

nicknamed 'platypuses', due to their bill-like slots, helped to speed the dispersal of tell-tale contrails.

The F-117 did not have conventional wings, but relied on the main fuselage for much of its lift. This is the 'lifting-body' or 'lifting-fuselage' concept, again not a new idea, as the Burnellis of the 1920s and '30s demonstrate, but a highly effective one. In fact, both Martin Marietta and Northrup were involved in lifting-body research during the 1960s, the objective here being not toward

LEFT & BELOW: The SR-71 is an advanced, long-range, Mach 3 strategic reconnaissance aircraft developed from the A-12 and YF-12A aircraft by the Lockheed Skunk Works. The SR-71 was unofficially named the Blackbird, but is referred to as the Habu by its crew.

military aircraft but to examine the feasibility of the space shuttle. Tiny research planes were built that bore no resemblance to the shuttle, but were part of what made it possible, by contributing a wealth of technical data

and understanding of the subject. In aircraft design, as in so many things, there is no substitute for leaving the

drawing board or computer screen and actually building something in order to see whether or not it will work.

The shuttle project was a joint NASA-U.S.A.F. programme, but Northrop's research partner was NASA

144

alone, whose first product was the M2-F1, an unmanned wooden glider used to test the concept of a lifting-body aircraft. This was soon followed by the M2-F2, still a glider but of metal construction and with a pilot. The fuselage was a D-shaped cross-section, its flat side uppermost, with flaps on the upper and lower surfaces for pitch-and-roll control and more on the fins for yaw control. In July 1966, it was launched mid-air from beneath the wing of a B-52, when it was able to make a successful controlled descent and landing.

Fourteen more glider flights followed until a Thiokol XLR II rocket motor of 8,480-lb thrust was fitted. But before it was even used, the little plane suffered serious damage after a wheels-up landing during another gliding test. It was later rebuilt as the M2-F3 with an extra central fin, and was used for powered tests between 1970 and 1972.

Alongside the M2-F2, although it was built slightly later, Northrop

OPPOSITE & BELOW: The Lockheed F-117 Nighthawk is a stealth ground-attack aircraft, formerly operated by the U.S. Air Force. The F-117A's first flight was in 1981, and it achieved Initial Operational Capability status in October 1983. The F-117A was 'acknowledged' and revealed to the world in November 1988.

designed the HL-10. Like its cousin, this was a tiny lifting-body single-seater. It too had a D-shaped cross-section, although it was the other way

around, with the flat side underneath, thus allowing the cockpit to be faired into the rounded topside. Right from the start it had a central fin and rudder, similar to that later fitted to the M2-F3, also the same XLR 11 rocket motor.

HL-10 made its first gliding test only a few months after M2-F2, and in five years completed 12 unpowered and 25 powered flights. It may have looked odd, but the HL-10 was a high-performance aircraft that could reach an altitude of over 90,000ft (27432m) and attain a speed of Mach 1.861. The Thiokol rocket was later replaced with three 500-lb (227-kg) Bell hydrogen-peroxide rockets. These could be started and run individually, giving a choice of three thrust levels to ascertain whether a space shuttle would need auxiliary power on the landing approach.

The Northrop HL-10 (seen opposite on the ground and below) was one of five heavyweight lifting-body designs flown at NASA's Flight Research Center from July 1966 to November 1975 to study and validate the concept of safely manoeuvring and landing a low, lift-over-drag vehicle designed for re-entry from space.

Space Shuttle mission STS-7 in June 1988, using NASA's Orbiter Challenger and carrying among its crew Sally Ride, the first U.S. woman to venture into space.

Meanwhile, the Martin Marietta company was also looking into lifting-body aircraft, and had been doing so independently since 1959. This time the customer was the U.S.A.F., which contracted the company to build four hypersonic unmanned (but controllable) craft to test re-entry into the atmosphere. Named SV-5D, this later became the X-23A, the first having been blasted into space on the back of an Atlas ballistic missile in December 1966. Three of these were launched, and gave valuable feedback on heat-shielding and manoeuvrability during re-entry.

Alongside these unmanned planes was the piloted X-24A, using the same XLR 111 motor as the Northrop M-series but with the addition of two Bell rocket motors. Like every other aircraft in the series, it made gliding tests first, from April 1969, with powered trials following over the next two years. It would eventually be rebuilt as the X-24B by Martin Marietta, making another 36 flights, both powered and as gliders, up to November 1975. But that wasn't the end of lifting-body research, and work continued into the late 20th century. One concept, another variation on the idea of a re-useable spacecraft, came from Lockheed Martin, and was the ability to carry an 18-tonne payload into low orbit at relatively low cost.

Flying wings, space shuttles and lifting bodies, all of them are just about recognizable as aircraft, but the Avrocar was something else. Just as the

world was going crazy about flying saucers, Avro Canada brought out the real thing. Making its first (tethered) flight in December 1959, the Avrocar was a circular craft that could take off and land vertically, as well as fly horizontally. There was a two-man crew, and three Continental J69 turbojets powered a central fan. This created an air cushion and a peripheral air curtain which supported the Avrocar in hover mode, while the main

The Martin Marietta X-24B, an experimental aircraft developed from a joint U.S.A.F.-NASA programme named PILOT (1963–75). It was designed and built to test lifting-body concepts, experimenting with the unpowered re-entry and landing later to be used by the Space Shuttle.

LEFT: The X-24A was flown 28 times in the programme that, like the HL-10, validated the concept that a Space Shuttle vehicle could be landed unpowered. The fastest speed achieved by the X-24A was 1,036mph (1667km/h or Mach 1.6). Its maximum altitude was 71,400ft (21.8km).

OPPOSITE: The VZ-9-AV Avrocar was a Canadian VTOL aircraft developed by Avro Aircraft Ltd. as part of a secret U.S. military project carried out in the early years of the Cold War. The Avrocar was intended to exploit the Coanda effect (the tendency of a fluid jet to stay attached to an adjacent curved surface) to provide lift and thrust from a single turborotor, blowing exhaust out of the rim of the disk-shaped aircraft to provide anticipated VTOL-like performance. In the air, it would have resembled a flying saucer.

body provided lift in level flight. It was tested at length and was eventually dropped, but the Avrocar did prove that at least one flying saucer (though of the terrestrial type) really did exist.

Another variation on the vertical take-off and landing (VTOL) theme was the Piasecki VZ-8 Aerial Geep, in which two 530-hp Turbomeca Artouste turboshaft engines drove two three-

bladed ducted rotors turning in opposite directions, that allowed the Geep to hover and make horizontal flights, while powered wheels meant that it could travel overland as well. It was intended, as the name suggests, to be an airborne version of the more familiar jeep, enabling its crew of two to undertake reconnaissance and observation missions. Two other research vehicles bore a passing resemblance to the Geep, though neither had its overland capability; both were nicknamed 'Flying Bedstead'. As early as 1953 Rolls-Royce's Flying Bedstead was being actively tested, research that eventually led to the Hawker Harrier jump jet. Much later, NASA's Lunar Landing Research Vehicle, designed to simulate moon landings, was given the same name. It later crashed, almost killing the pilot, who just happened to be Neil Armstrong.

OPPOSITE: This 1964 photograph shows the Lunar Landing Research Vehicle (LLRV), affectionately dubbed the 'Flying Bedstead', in flight at Edwards Air Force Base in California. NASA used the LLRV to simulate the Apollo lunar landings.

BELOW: The Piasecki VZ-8 Aerial Geep, another variation on the VTOL theme.

CHAPTER FIVE

UPPERS & DOWNERS

During the Second World War, those piloting the fastest fighters noticed something strange happening when making high-speed dives. The plane would begin to shudder, buffeting around as if encountering severe turbulence. As speed increased, it would become more and more difficult to control, and P-38 Lightning pilots found their aircraft difficult to pull out of fast dives, while the Spitfire suffered from 'roll reversal', in which wing-flex would counteract control input at the ailerons. In extreme cases, the aircraft would actually break up.

This was caused by the airflow becoming transonic over the wings as the aircraft approached supersonic speeds. It was not fully understood at the time, and the dramatic aerodynamic effects led to the 'sound barrier' description, as if it were a wall as solid as that of a house and as difficult to smash through. In the closing stages of the war, a Messerschmitt Me 262 pilot claimed to have actually broken

through the sound barrier and to have flown supersonically, although his account was later discredited, for at that speed a traditional airspeed indicator would have overread due to shock waves.

Not that supersonic flight hadn't been achieved. Germany's V-2 ballistic missiles had gone supersonic in 1942, and were routinely achieving Mach 4

two years later. But these were unmanned, and the aim of designers was to build a manned aircraft that could break the sound barrier, be controllable at supersonic speeds, and land safely. In this, the British led the field for a short time, and at the behest of the Air Ministry, Miles Aircraft began research into building such a plane in 1942.

This was the M-52, which had many features that would later become standard on supersonic aircraft, such as an all-moving tailplane to maintain control once the sound barrier had

been broached. Powered by a turbojet engine with afterburner, the M-52 was designed to achieve 1,000mph (1610km/h) in a dive from 36,000ft (10970m). Its wings were very thin and straight, because it was known that conventional thick wings were more vulnerable to sound-barrier shock waves. But the M-52 never flew, and the project was cancelled in 1946, partly because of spending cuts and partly because information garnered from captured German research indicated that swept-back, rather than straight, wings were essential for supersonic

flight. In the event, the latter proved to be spurious, and a three tenths-scale unmanned model of the M-52 was able to achieve Mach 1.5 in October 1948. There is little doubt that the M-52 would have successfully broken the sound barrier if it had flown, despite its straight wings.

The Soviets, incidentally, were researching into supersonic flight at the same time. Like the Allies, they benefited greatly from captured German research and aeronautical specialists. German engineers taken east, not always voluntarily, continued work on their swept-wing DFS 346 from October 1946, which was subsequently tested in both glider and powered forms.

A full year before the model M-52 broke the sound barrier, Charles 'Chuck' Yeager had already made the

OPPOSITE ABOVE: Chuck Yeager at the controls of the cramped cockpit of a Bell X-1, named Glamorous Glennis after his wife.

OPPOSITE BELOW: The underside of a Bell X-1.

ABOVE: The first Bell XS-1 (X-1), used in the world's first supersonic flight.

The North American X-15 rocket-powered aircraft was part of the American X-series of experimental aircraft, initiated with the Bell X-1. The X-15 set numerous speed and altitude records in the early 1960s, reaching the edge of space and bringing back valuable data that was used in the design of later aircraft and spacecraft.

first official supersonic manned flight. As part of a wartime agreement between the Allies, the British had sent the results of their supersonic research to the United States, expecting the Americans to reciprocate. Unfortunately for Britain's aircraft industry, they did not, and U.S. research into the field, begun in 1943,

was kept secret. In March 1945 Bell Aircraft was awarded a contract to build three research aircraft capable of breaking the sound barrier. The XS-1 had a bullet-shaped fuselage and straight wings only 3.5-in (9-cm) thick, and was built strongly enough to resist the 10-g forces involved. The first gliding test was made in January 1946,

North American Aviation's B-70 Valkyrie was a nuclear-armed bomber designed for the U.S. Air Force's Strategic Air Command in the 1950s. The Valkyrie was a large six-engined aircraft, able to fly at Mach 3 at high altitudes, which would have allowed it to avoid defending interceptors, the only effective anti-bomber weapon at the time.

and a powered flight followed at the end of that year. The X-1, or 'Glamorous Glennis', as it became known, was kept busy, and made its 50th flight in October 1947. Launched from the belly of a B-29, with Chuck Yeager at the controls, it attained Mach 1.06 at 42,000ft (12800m) in the world's first recognized manned

supersonic flight. The speed records tumbled from then on as an X-1 reached Mach 1.45 soon afterwards, and a second-generation plane (also termed X-1) managed Mach 2.435 in December 1953. Within a few years, production combat aircraft were breaking the sound barrier; therefore, manned supersonic flight came very

The Douglas X-3 Stiletto was a 1950s U.S. experimental jet aircraft with a slender fuselage and a long tapered nose. Its primary mission was to investigate the design features of an aircraft suitable for sustained supersonic speeds, which included the first use of titanium in major airframe components. It was, however, seriously underpowered for its purpose, and was unable even to exceed Mach 1 in level flight.

quickly, regardless of whomever had done the original research, or had made the running in their development.

While Bell and Chuck Yeager were earning their places in the history books, due to the X-1, Douglas Aircraft was building its own experimental supersonic plane, the long, thin X-3 Stiletto. This first flew in October 1952, having been designed to reach Mach 3, but which turned out to be something of a disappointment

in that it achieved a mere Mach 0.95 in level flight over 20 missions. It was also intended that the X-3 should not only provide data on the use of turbojets, which were more practical than rocket motors for reuse, but also on short 'double-edged' wings. The engineers also wished to discover more about thermodynamic heating at such high speeds, one of the side-effects of supersonic flight being the immense friction of air rushing over the surface

of the aircraft and heating it to a high temperature.

Whatever the research uses of the X-3, in terms of sheer speed it was eclipsed by a Bell X-2, that exceeded Mach 3 in September 1956. But even this was overshadowed by the latest research plane, the X-15. Like the earlier Bell X-series, this was rocket-powered, first by two XLR 11s and later by a single 57,000-lb thrust XLR 99. Making its first flight as an unpowered glider in June 1959, the X-15 was certainly fast, but it was also intended to deliver data on control,

stability and heating at extreme altitudes. It flew so high, reaching 354,200ft (107960m) in August 1963, or a height of almost 67 miles (108km), that its pilots could be termed astronauts. Four years later, exactly two decades after Chuck Yeager's first supersonic flight, the X-15 was able to touch Mach 6.72.

With such prodigious speeds attainable by research aircraft, and production fighters already flying supersonically, the next step for the U.S. military was to contemplate a supersonic bomber. Intended to replace

The Tupolev Tu-144 was the first supersonic transport aircraft (SST), constructed under the direction of the Soviet Tupolev design bureau headed by Alexei Tupolev. Some Western observers nicknamed the plane Concordski, as the Tu-144 bore a resemblance to the Anglo-French Concorde. A prototype first flew on 31 December 1968 near Moscow, two months before Concorde. The Tu-144 first broke the sound barrier on 5 June 1969, and on 15 July 1969 became the first commercial transport to exceed Mach 2, making it the fastest commercial airliner in existence at that time.

WEIRD AIRCRAFT

The Aérospatiale-BAC Concorde, a supersonic passenger airliner, was a product of an Anglo-French government treaty, combining the manufacturing efforts of Aérospatiale and the British Aircraft Corporation. With only 20 aircraft ultimately built, the costly development phase represented a substantial economic loss. Additionally, Air France and British Airways were subsidized by their governments to buy the aircraft. The Concorde was the more successful of the only two supersonic airliners to have ever operated commercially, the Tupolev Tu-144 being the other. The Tu-144 was also the only faster commercial airliner, surpassing the Concorde by 100mph (161km/h).

the venerable B-52, design work on the XB-70A Valkyrie got under way during the early 1960s, though in 1963 changes in strategy, not to mention budget cuts, meant it was no longer needed as a bomber. Nevertheless, work went ahead to build two prototypes for further aerodynamic research.

One of these first flew in September 1964, its 105-ft (32-m) span delta wings equipped with hydraulically controlled drooping wingtips and 12 trailing-edge elevons. It was powered by six 31,000-lb thrust General Electric YJ93-GE-3

turbojets, which enabled it to meet its design speed of Mach 3. The second prototype was completed and also flew, but it collided with a chase plane in 1966 and was destroyed.

So if larger supersonic aircraft were possible, why not supersonic airliners as well? Flying at Mach 1 or 2 promised drastically reduced travel times on long-haul flights, halving the time of a transatlantic trip. In the event, the Russian Tupolev Tu-144 was abandoned after suffering a disastrous crash at the Paris Air Show.

The Anglo-French Concorde was in commercial service for two decades and was a technological success, though in reality its benefits were restricted to the super-rich, who could afford to pay a supersonic fare for the privilege of flying in it.

WHIRLYBIRDS

While Leonardo da Vinci may have built a tiny model of a helicopter all those centuries ago, helicopters as practical flying machines arrived relatively late. Even during the 1920s only short flights were made, and pure helicopters were unable to match the performance of autogyros. The breakthrough came with the German Focke-Wulf Fw-61 (*page*

167), which flew successfully in 1937, breaking all helicopter flight records, while the following year, the famous test pilot, Hannah Reitsch, became the first woman to fly a helicopter. A twin-rotor Focke-Achgelis Fa 266 followed, intended as a transport, but in the midst of war only a few were in fact built.

Meanwhile, on the other side of the Atlantic, Igor Sikorsky's simple single-rotor R-4 did make it into production, and 131 were built for the U.S. military from 1944. By the end of the war, Sikorsky had built over 400 machines, the Bell 47 arriving soon afterwards as the first relatively simple, reliable helicopter, that made it a huge commercial success.

But it is the incredible and extraordinary that interest us here. The

OPPOSITE: *Paul Cornu in his first helicopter in 1907. Note that he is sitting between the two rotors, which rotated in opposite directions to cancel torque. This helicopter was the first flying machine to rise from the ground using rotor blades instead of wings.*

ABOVE: *The Bréguet-Richet gyroplane of 1907.*

Piasecki PV-3, better known as the 'Flying Banana' (*page 168*), was the first successful machine with tandem rotors, which first flew in March 1945 and saw service with the U.S. Navy and Marine Corps from 1947. The Flying Banana, of course, had its twin rotors driven by the engine, as had all previous helicopters, but the Hughes XH-17 (*page 169*) was different in this

respect. Not only did it have the largest rotor ever fitted to an engine-powered helicopter, but at 130ft (40m) it was also driven by gas pressure, the exhaust gases from two General Electric GE 5500 turbojets passing through hollow ducts in the rotors to exit at the tips. It was an elegant idea that dispensed with the need for heavy and mechanically inefficient transmission. It was a

ABOVE: The 1915 Austrian Petroczy-Karman-Zurovec PKZ 2 helicopter with Gnôme Monosoupape engine. This first version did not carry personnel.

massive machine, with a gross weight of 50,000lbs (22680kg) and the capability of lifting 15 tonnes; it was hardly surprising that the craft earned the

OPPOSITE: Raúl Pateras Pescara's No. 3 helicopter was built in 1923 and by January 1924 was capable of making flights of some ten minutes' duration.

The Focke-Achgelis Fa 223 Drache (Dragon) was a helicopter developed by Germany during the Second World War, and was the first such machine to attain production status.

nickname the 'Flying Crane'. It first flew in October 1952, but never got beyond the prototype stage, as a result of which this sole example was eventually scrapped.

Frank Piasecki was still working on helicopter research for the U.S. military, and a much later prototype was the vectored-thrust combat-agility demonstrator (VTCAD). This consisted

The Focke-Wulf Fw 61 was the first fully controllable helicopter, and made its first flight in 1936. It is more properly known as the Fa 61, it being a research aircraft of the Focke-Achgelis company.

of a vectored-thrust pusher propeller, mounted on the rear of an Apache or SuperCobra helicopter fuselage, and was reminiscent of the Lockheed AH-56A Cheyenne, an attack helicopter with pusher propeller that very nearly made it into full-scale production. With a General Electric T64-GE-16 engine driving both the main rotor and a pusher propeller, it was able to combine the VTOL attributes of a helicopter with a level flight speed of 253mph (407km/h). The U.S. Army ordered 375 of these machines in 1968, but changed its mind the following year and cancelled the order.

OPPOSITE: The Piasecki HRP Rescuer was a U.S. tandem-rotor transport or rescue helicopter, designed by Frank Piasecki and initially built as the PV-3 development aircraft, affectionately known as 'The Flying Banana', and subsequently produced for the U.S. Navy and U.S. Coast Guard as the HRP-1 Rescuer. An improved PV-17 variant was produced as the HRP-2.

RIGHT: The XH-17 'Flying Crane' was the first project of the helicopter division of Hughes Aircraft. The XH-17, which had a two-bladed main rotor system with a diameter of 134ft (41m), was capable of flying at a gross weight of more than 50,000lbs (22680kg).

RIGHT BELOW: The Cierva C. 6c, built in 1926 by Avro. It was powered by a 130-hp Clerget engine and incorporated an Avro 504 fuselage.

HELICOPTERS-AND-A-HALF

The pusher-propeller Cheyenne was only one of a long line of research aircraft intended to combine the convenience of a helicopter with the speed and range of a fixed-wing plane. But while the Cheyenne was a modified helicopter, many others were true hybrids, and countless man-hours were

OPPOSITE: *The Cierva W.11 Air Horse, a British 1940s helicopter that was the largest in the world when it first flew in 1948.*

BELOW: *The 1934 Cierva C.30 marked a major step forward in rotorcraft development.*

expended before such craft finally achieved success. The Rolls-Royce 'Flying Bedstead' of the mid-1950s (*page 177*) has already been mentioned, whose official title was the Thrust Measuring Rig, in that the exhaust ducts of its two Rolls-Royce Nene

engines were turned downwards by 90 degrees to deliver the required vertical thrust.

Only a few years later, the world's first large VTOL aircraft appeared, the Fairey Rotodyne (*page 176*), another British research project that used two

Napier Eland 3000-hp turboprop engines to drive both the twin main propellers and the 90-ft (27-m) rotor. The propellers were driven in the conventional way, but the rotor turned via an engine-driven compressor, which supplied compressed air to the rotor

tips. It was similar to the system used in the exhaust-driven Hughes XH-17 rotor, but in this case fuel was added at the tips to create the thrust.

Intended as a transport plane, the Rotodyne Y was capable of carrying 40 passengers, and was able to take off

ABOVE: The Kaman K-225 Mixmaster, in service with the U.S. Coast Guard from 1950–54.

OPPOSITE: The collapsible Dornier Do 32 jet helicopter could be folded and stored in a box to be transported in a car trailer.

LEFT: The Fairey Gyrodyne became the world's fastest helicopter by breaking the new International Speed Record for helicopters on 28 June 1948.

BELOW LEFT: The Soviet-made Mil Mi-12 (also known as the V-12) is the largest helicopter ever built. It features the only two-rotor transverse scheme ever produced by Mil, thus eliminating the need for a tail rotor. The twin engines were taken together with the rotors from the Mil Mi-6 and duplicated on the Mi-12.

OPPOSITE: The 1947 McDonnell XH-20 Little Henry Research Helicopter. Sponsored by the U.S. Army Air Forces/U.S. Air Force, Little Henry proved that helicopters could fly using ramjets located in the tips of their rotor blades, the tip-driven rotor eliminating the need for a torque-compensating tail rotor. It did not need a transmission and was controlled by neans of a rudder.

vertically using the rotor, with the propellers taking over once it had gained sufficient horizontal speed, by which time the wings, not the rotor, would be providing the lift. The Rotodyne made its first flight in November 1957, and five months later

made its first transition to horizontal flight. It had great protential, and there was commercial interest in the design, but the British government put an end to the project in 1962.

At around the same time, a number of companies in the U.S.A. and mainland Europe were experimenting using different techniques, such as deflected slipstream or deflected propellers. These did away with the need for a helicopter rotor, and in the case of the former used large wing flaps literally

OPPOSITE: The British Fairey Rotodyne was intended for commercial and military applications in the 1950s and early 1960s. A development of the earlier Fairey Gyrodyne prototypes, which had established a number of British helicopter records, the Rotodyne featured a jet-tipped powered rotor, burning fuel with compressed air bled from two wingtip-mounted Napier Eland turboprops. The rotor was used for vertical take-offs, landings and hovering, while full power was applied to the tractor propellers of the turboprops when engaged in forward flight.

RIGHT: Rolls-Royce's twin Nene-powered Flying Bedstead (Thrust Measuring Rig), under test in 1953.

to deflect the thrust of the otherwise conventional propellers sufficiently to allow short or vertical take-offs. The American version was the Fairchild VZ-5FA. A 1024-hp General Electric turboshaft engine drove four propellers,

and for a vertical take-off the aircraft sat with its nose in the air at an angle of 45 degrees. It made a tethered flight in November 1959.

In France, the Bréguet 940 Intégral (*page 184*) had successfully flown the

previous year, though it had been designed for short rather than true vertical take-offs. Four Turbomeca Turmo turboshaft engines drove three-blade propellers, whose slipstream was blasted over the wings and their

OPPOSITE: The Fairchild VZ-5FA, making a tethered vertical flight.

ABOVE & PAGES 180–181: The Dornier Do 29 experimental aircraft had extreme STOL capability, its engines pivoted for maximum vertical thrust.

double-slotted flaps. Four Intégrals were built and supplied to the French Armée de l'Air.

By contrast, Dornier preferred the deflected propeller approach, at least at first. The Do 29, which first flew late in 1958, was powered by two 270-hp

Lycoming piston engines, which could pivot, complete with their propellers, by up to 90 degrees to produce vertical thrust. Dornier's later Do 31E (*page 182*), intended as a transport plane with room for cargo or 34 troops, was different again; each wing carried a

15,500lb-thrust Rolls-Royce Pegasus 5-2 vectored engine, with a removable pod at the wingtip encasing four 4,400lb-thrust RB lift jets. Thus equipped, the Do 31E made its first take-off in February 1967, making the transition from vertical to horizontal flight shortly before Christmas the same year. As with so many other projects, this showed great promise for both military and civilian use. Many test flights were made, although it ultimately failed to reach production.

Another variation, intended to achieve the same ends, was the EWR VJ 101C, another jet-powered VTOL machine, which was meant to form the basis of a Mach 2 fighter, and had six engines in all. First and most obvious were the pods on each wingtip, each containing a pair of 2,750-lb (1247-kg) Rolls-Royce RB 145 turbojets, the pods swivelling to allow them to act as lift or horizontal jets. Another two engines, designed to act only as lift jets, were mounted vertically in the fuselage. The first prototype made a hovering flight in April 1963, took off conventionally in August, and made its first transition from vertical to horizontal flight (the moment of truth for any VTOL prototype) a month later. It could

exceed Mach 1 in horizontal flight, but after slowing to 190mph (306km/h), the wingtip pods tilted to 45 degrees; at 57mph (92km/h), they reached a full 90-degree tilt, providing lift so that the aircraft could slow to a stop and hover.

TILTING WINGS
Helicopters, autogyros, jet-propelled rotors, deflected slipstream and deflecting propellers, all were means by which a proven V/STOL aircraft could be produced. But there was yet another method: the tilting wing. This was pioneered by the Boeing Vertol VZ-2A of 1957, and was followed by larger machines. The Fairchild X-18 came only two years later, based on the existing Chase YC-122 transport aircraft, fitted with two Allison T40 turboprop engines with Curtiss-Wright contra-rotating propellers. It was never intended to be anything more than a flying testbed, but perhaps the X-18's most important legacy was that it led to the development of the XC-142 (*page 189*).

This was the joint effort of three manufacturers, LTV, Hiller and Ryan, under the general auspices of the U.S.A.F. The concept was for a cargo plane, able to carry troops or supplies into hostile terrain where no landing-

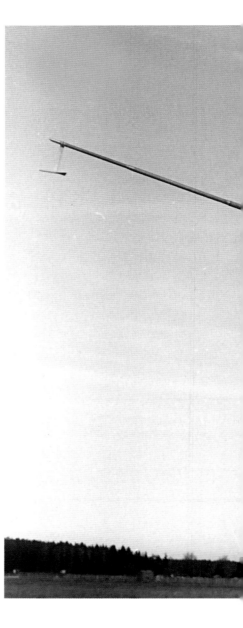

ABOVE & LEFT: The Dornier Do 31 jet transport. Forward power and some lift was provided by the two Rolls-Royce Pegasus 5-2 engines, with VTOL capability provided by four RB-162-4 lift engines in each wingtip pod.

OPPOSITE: The Bell Model 65 Air Test Vehicle (ATV) was constructed with existing components. The wing was from a Cessna 170, the fuselage from a Schweizer glider, and the fixed undercarriage skids came from the Bell Model 47 helicopter. These combined into a parasol-wing monoplane, with a T-tail and two small Fairchild turbojets added.

strip was available. It would have to be capable both of vertical take-off from a land base or assault ship, and landing in difficult conditions. The tilting wing would move through 100 degrees to give vertical thrust, carrying with it four 2850-hp turboprop engines.

Trials of the first of five prototypes began in September 1964, with the first hover test completed at the end of the year and a transition from vertical to horizontal flight a few weeks later. In May 1966, trials on the aircraft carrier USS *Bennington* were

under way, and by all accounts the various tests went well, sufficiently so for the U.S.A.F. to seek details of a production version; in the end, however, the finance was not forthcoming and the XC-142A was able to proceed no further.

OPPOSITE: The Bréguet 940 Intégral.

BELOW· The EWR VJ 101 was an experimental German VTOL jet fighter. It was to be the basis for a successor to the F-104G Starfighter, but was cancelled in 1968 after a five-year test programme. The VJ 101 was one of the first V/STOL designs to have the potential for eventual Mach 2 flight.

The same fate befell the Canadian Canadair CL-84 (*pages 190 and 191*), developed at the same time as the XC. Much smaller than the U.S. aircraft, it was intended for the same sort of military role, transporting 16 troops and/or cargo to wherever they were needed. It used two 1400-hp Lycoming T53 turboshaft engines, mounted on wings which could tilt 100 degrees.

Canadair predicted a top speed of over 320mph (515km/h), which would have made the CL-84 usefully fast as well as adaptable. The testing went well, and the first prototype amassed 405 hours of flying time over 305 flights, resulting in a prototype that had been more thoroughly trialled than most. The first CL-84 was destroyed in a crash, but an improved CL-84-1 was developed and

OPPOSITE & BELOW: The Boeing Vertol VZ-2 (Model 76), a research aircraft built in the United States in 1957 to investigate the tilting-wing approach to vertical take-off and landing. The aircraft had a fuselage of tubular framework (originally uncovered) and accommodated its pilot in a helicopter-like bubble canopy.

three prototypes were built. The first of these was flown in 1970 and again underwent testing, but still no full-scale production was initiated.

The concept of tilting wings was evidently a promising one, but none of these prototypes was able to make the final leap into series-production

operational aircraft, although the manufacturers had sincerely hoped that they would. Bell, on the other hand, had no such ambitions for its X-22A (*page 192*), which was being developed at the same time as these tilting-wing planes. This had neither tilting wings, and despite the helicopter-style

ABOVE & RIGHT: The forerunner of the XC-142, the Hiller X-18 was an experimental cargo transport aircraft, designed to be the first testbed for tilt-wing and STOVL (short take off and vertical landing) technology.

OPPOSITE: The Ling-Temco-Vought (LTV) XC-142, a tilt-wing experimental aircraft designed to investigate the operational suitability of V/STOL transports.

fuselage, nor did it have a rotor. Instead, large ducts from all four engines could be tilted through 95 degrees at a rate of five degrees per second. Each one had an elevon control

surface in its slipstream, and power came from four 1250-hp General Electric YT58-GE-8D turboshafts, each driving a three-blade propeller mounted in one of the tilting ducts.

The X-22A was first flown in March 1966, and like the Canadair CL-84 was thoroughly tested, its two prototypes between them making hundreds of flights. The X-22A

189

proved capable of vertical take-offs, short take-offs, horizontal flights and made a stable transition between modes. Anticipated as a pure research aircraft, this four-engined Bell was still being flown right up to 1984, which for a research machine was very good going indeed.

Before the X-22A came off the drawing board, there being no reliance on computers in those days, Bell already had a different form of V/STOL aircraft up and running. The XV-3 (*page 195*) had first flown in August 1955, and was much smaller than any of the above prototypes, with seating for only four and a single Pratt & Whitney R-985 piston engine providing the power. Its

OPPOSITE & BELOW: The Canadair CL-84 was a V/STOL turbine tilt-wing monoplane designed and manufactured by Canadair between 1964 and 1972. Only four of these experimental aircraft were built, with three entering flight testing. Two of the CL-84s crashed due to mechanical failures, but no loss of life occurred as a result of these accidents.

unique feature was the wingtip rotors, which could be tilted vertically or horizontally according to need. They could be more properly described as proprotors, in that they fulfilled the functions of both propellers and rotors, depending on whether the XV-3 was flying horizontally or vertically. Its propellers were large in proportion with

the wingspan, being of 33-ft (10-m) diameter against a 31-ft wingspan, a side-effect of which was that helicopter mode was required when landing.

The XV-3 proved a competent aircraft, able to achieve 181mph (291km/h) in level flight, and tilt its proprotors fully in 10–15 seconds. Two such machines were built, which made

ABOVE & RIGHT: The Bell X-22A was a U.S. V/STOL X-plane with four tilting ducted fans. Take-off was to selectively occur either with the propellers tilted vertically upwards, or on a short runway with the nacelles tilted forward at approximately 45 degrees. Additionally, the X-22 was to provide more insight into the tactical application of VTOL troop transporters, such as the preceding Hiller X-18 and the XV-15 successor.

over 250 flights, proving themselves to be useful research tools. Bell would resurrect the proprotor idea in 1977 for the XV-15 (*page 196*), another pure research aircraft, but it wasn't until 1989 that a more serious project was initiated once more.

This was the V-22 Osprey, a joint venture between Bell and Boeing. Like its predecessors, it was a twin-proprotor machine, although much

larger, but unlike these aircraft was intended for mass-production. What they may not have known then was just how long this process would take. The two 38-ft (11.6-m) proprotors were driven by two 6150-hp Allison T406-AD-400 turboshaft engines, enabling it to take off and land vertically, reach 361mph (581km/h), and carry a nine-tonne load for over 2,000 miles (3220km).

But the Osprey's journey toward production had been long and fraught. The programme had begun back in 1981 as a joint-services project, initially led by the U.S. Army, for a multi-function machine able to undertake a multiplicity of roles, including troop and cargo transport, assault, medical evacuation, search and rescue, and special operations. Full-scale development began five years later and the Osprey

OPPOSITE: The Nord 500 ducted-propeller research aircraft, hovering in tethered flight with its two 317-shp Allison turboshaft engines in the vertical position.

BELOW: The Bell XV-3 (Bell 200), a tiltrotor aircraft first flown in 1955. Like its predecessors, the XV-3 had its engines in the fuselage, and driveshafts transferring power out to tilting wingtip rotor assemblies.

UPPERS & DOWNERS

The Bell Boeing XV-15 was the second successful experimental tiltrotor VTOL aircraft and the first to demonstrate the concept's high-speed performance relative to conventional helicopters.

made its first vertical flight in March 1989, with horizontal flight the following September. Sea trials aboard the USS *Wasp* followed in 1990, but one of the six prototypes crashed on a

demonstration flight in 1992, killing everyone on board. All further testing was suspended, and did not restart until 1993 after changes had been made.

Testing continued into the late 1990s on pre-production machines, but it wasn't until 2005 that the operational tests were finally complete and the go-ahead could be given for full production. In the meantime, two more fatal crashes had occurred in 2000, leading *Time* magazine to conclude

The Bell Boeing V-22 Osprey, a joint-service, multi-mission military tiltrotor aircraft, with both VTOL and STOL capabilities.

that the Osprey was unsafe, overpriced and totally inadequate, although it was strongly defended by the Marine Corps. Costs had also spiralled, and the V-22's 25-year development period had swallowed $20 billion, with each

The Bell Boeing V-22 Osprey tiltrotor, showing the flight sequence of the rotors.

production aircraft costing $70 million. Plans went ahead for an eventual production of over 450, nevertheless, making the Osprey the only proprotor machine, at the time of writing, to make it onto the factory floor.

FAST VTOLS

Most of the tilting-engine, tilting-wing and proprotor prototypes had one thing in common in that they were not high-speed aircraft, which was why military interest concentrated on their suitability in the transport role rather than as bombers or fighters. But there have been several attempts to build a versatile V/STOL fixed-wing fighter, of which the Hawker Siddeley Harrier, later produced jointly between British Aerospace and McDonnell Douglas, is the most well-known and certainly the most successful and long-lived. The Harrier, of course, used a single jet engine, its exhaust exiting through four vectoring thrust nozzles to provide vertical or horizontal thrust and a transition between the two.

The experimental Lockheed XFV-1 Salmon, a tail-sitting fighter.

LEFT & OPPOSITE: The Convair XFY Pogo tail-sitter was an experiment in vertical take-off and landing. The Pogo had delta wings and three-bladed contra-rotating propellers powered by a 5850-hp Allison YT40-A-16 turboprop engine. It was intended to be a high-performance fighter aircraft, capable of operating from small warships. Landing the XFY was difficult as the pilot had to look over his shoulder while carefully working the throttle to land.

But V/STOL fighters had been under development long before the Harrier came on the scene. In 1950, the U.S. Navy had been keen to have access to a fighter that could take off vertically from a small platform, instead of from a large carrier deck, allowing it to operate from smaller ships, and held a design competition to this effect. Both Lockheed and Convair were awarded contracts to produce prototypes, and Lockheed's XFV-1 Salmon and Convair's XFY-1 Pogo proved remarkably similar.

Both were tail-sitters, in that they sat vertically, tail on the ground, supported by castor-wheels on legs attached to the wings' trailing-edges. Both used the same Allison YT40

turboprop engine with the equivalent of 5850hp, driving Curtiss-Wright Turboelectric co-axial contra-rotating propellers. Armament, in the form of guns or rockets, was carried in wingtip pods and the pilot's seat had the facility to tilt according to the flight mode.

The safest way to test these tail-sitters was by means of tethered flights, and many were made, using a special test rig inside a naval airship hangar. The Lockheed was the first to make a free flight, in March 1954, but only horizontally, with temporary landing gear added so that it could also land in that mode. But the U.S. Navy was not impressed, and terminated the Salmon project shortly afterwards. The Convair Pogo fared rather better. Its first free

LEFT & OPPOSITE BELOW: The Ryan X-13 Vertijet (Model 69), an experimental VTOL aircraft flown in the U.S. in the 1950s. The main objective was to demonstrate the ability of a pure jet to vertically take off, hover, transition to horizontal forward flight, and vertically land.

OPPOSITE ABOVE: The Lockheed XFV-1 was the first vehicle capable of high-speed, straight-up flight.

OPPOSITE: The Bristol Siddeley Pegasus-powered P 1127 V/STOL strike aircraft.

BELOW: The French Dassault Mirage IIIV VTOL fighter. Unlike its predecessor, the Dassault Mirage III, the IIIV model featured eight small vertical lift jets straddling the main engine. The design came in response to a mid-1960s NATO specification for a VTOL strike fighter.

flight was a vertical one, in August 1954, and it went on to make 70 more vertical take-offs and landings, making the mid-air transition to horizontal flight in November the same year. But although the Pogo was a true VTOL, and could reach 500mph (800km/h), it had problems of stability, among others, that also led to its cancellation.

But if Lockheed and Convair had been unable to deliver the goods,

perhaps Ryan, another U.S. manufacturer, could. Ryan had a good basis for building a VTOL jet fighter. It had been researching jet-boosted, piston-engined fighters since 1943, one of which actually went into production. The FR-1 Fireball (*page 92*) was Ryan's Model 28 piston-engined fighter, with the addition of a turbojet booster engine, and saw service with the U.S. Navy in 1945–47. This, in turn, led to

the XF2R-1, an experimental fighter with a turboprop engine in the nose and a turbojet in the tail, plus an impressive thrust-to-weight ratio of more than 1:1.

So the navy turned to Ryan in its search for a pure jet-powered VTOL, the company's response being the delta-winged X-13 Vertijet (*page 202*).

Powered by a 10,000lb-thrust Rolls-Royce Avon turbojet, it could take off vertically, like the Salmon and Pogo, even though its first flight in December 1955 was a horizontal one. Its first hovering flight came in May the following year, with a transition to horizontal (and back again) the

OPPOSITE: The Yakovlev Yak-141 Freestyle, a supersonic VTOL fighter aircraft from the Soviet Union.

BELOW: The Short SC.1 was the first British fixed-wing VTOL aircraft. It was designed as a test aircraft for the Rolls-Royce RB 108 vertical-lift turbojet engine.

following November. In April 1957 it succeeded in combining all modes in one flight when it took off vertically, made a transition, and followed this with a vertical landing. In short, the Vertijet was a success.

There had also been a British VTOL, prior to the Harrier, although the Short Brothers SC.1 had been intended as a research aircraft. It was closer to the Harrier in concept than any of the U.S. examples, in that it had a conventional undercarriage and was designed to take off and land vertically and also make conventional landings if desired. Construction began in 1954 and the first flight came three years later; but it wasn't until April 1960 that the SC.1 was able to make its first transition from vertical to horizontal flight.

Unlike the single-engined Harrier, the SC.1 had five, all of them 2,130-lb (966-kg) Rolls-Royce RB108 turbojets. Four were installed vertically in the fuselage, although they were able to tilt slightly to aid braking and forward thrust; the fifth was installed horizontally, being exclusively for forward thrust. Stability was ensured by using high-pressure air nozzles at the wingtips, tail and nose by way of a bleed from the engine compressors.

At around the same time, a French VTOL project was also in progress, though like the Short SC.1, the SNECMA Coléoptère was a pure research vehicle. It was a tail-sitter, like the American projects, but in this case looked as if it had been formed from the front half of a jet fighter married with the rear of a much larger missile. It made a first successful free vertical flight in May 1959, but was lost while attempting to make the transition to the horizontal the following July; the pilot escaped via his ejector seat.

TRANSPORTATION FOR ONE
The Bell Rocket- and Jet-Belts were very different forms of VTOL aircraft. The story goes that Bell engineer, Wendell Moore, sketched out the initial idea for the jet-belt in the sand at Edwards Airforce Base. What appeared in 1953 was a strap-on back-pack, intended to lift a man into the air and carry him a short distance. Fortunately, it was extensively rig-tested before it was strapped to a human being, but even then it was discovered that the jet nozzles had been placed too close to

The Harrier GR Mk 3 V/STOL close-support and reconnaissance aircraft.

209

LEFT & BELOW: The SNECMA Coléoptère was a VTOL aircraft developed by the French in the 1950s. It was a single-person aircraft, with an annular wing designed to land vertically, therefore requiring no runway and very little space to take off and land. Several prototypes were developed and tested, but the design proved to be unstable, making flying it potentially dangerous.

OPPOSITE: A pair of V/STOL Harrier II AV-8B aircraft of the U.S. Marine Corps on a training exercise.

the pilot, thus burning off the sleeves of his jacket.

Officially known as a Small Rocket Lift Device (SRLD). the jet-belt attracted military interest, the army warming to the idea of a back-pack that could fly infantry over minefields and rivers; in 1960 the U.S. Transportation, Research and Engineering Command awarded Bell a contract to develop it into a working system. Aerojet developed a variable-thrust rocket motor specifically for the jet-belt, although it still weighed a hefty 280lb (127kg). In April 1961 Harold Graham took the first untethered flight, which lasted only 13 seconds. The controls were simple. with a right-hand throttle and left-hand yaw control, and

In the early 1960s, Bell Aerosystems built a rocket pack which it called the Rocket-Belt or 'man-rocket' for the U.S. Army. The Rocket-Belt was powered by a hydrogen-peroxide reaction rocket engine, which consisted of a tank of compressed liquid nitrogen which pushed hydrogen peroxide out of two other tanks into a reaction chamber. There, a chemical reaction created an extremely hot, high-pressure stream, that escaped from the flight nozzles and propelled both unit and pilot.

BELOW & PAGES 214–215: The Saunders-Roe SR.A/1 jet flying-boat fighter TG263, the first and only prototype to survive the programme.

soon the SRLD was making far longer flights of up to 860ft (262m), attaining a height of 60ft (18m) and speeds of up to 60mph (100km/h). In one memorable demonstration, an SRLD pilot took off from an amphibious craft and landed in

front of President Kennedy, whom he presumably saluted smartly before taking off again.

Developed at the same time as the SRLD, the Hiller VZ-1 Do-Nut flying platform was capable of VTOL

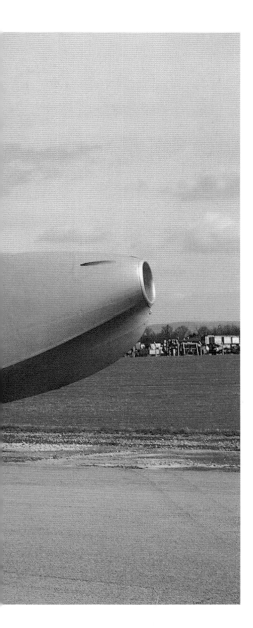

with one infantryman. Neither this nor the jet-belt went into production, even though the U.S. Army did contract Bell to develop it further, this time using a Williams turbojet, which promised a much longer flying time than the rocket motor. It successfully flew in April 1969 but failed to be adopted.

ULTIMATE SEAPLANES

If there is one place where the military is more vulnerable to attack than anywhere else it is on the ground. But it is not only the loss of aircraft but also the fact that accurate bombing can swiftly put an airfield out of action altogether. Taxiing or parked-up aircraft on runways make very easy targets, as the Soviet Union discovered to its cost on 22 June 1941, when Hitler ordered his land and air forces to make a ferocious attack. On that first day, 1,811 Soviet aircraft were lost, of which, incredibly, 1,489 (over 80 per cent) were on the ground.

The answer to the problem is to do without an airfield altogether, either by using VTOL aircraft or by basing aircraft on water. The ability to land on and take off from water also means that airstrips, prepared in advance, are no longer needed. It was advantages such as these that led British manufacturer, Saunders-Roe, to propose a single-seater jet-powered flying-boat fighter in 1943, and it received the go-ahead from the Air Ministry the following year.

The SR.A/1's single-step hull clearly distinguished it as an amphibious plane, but it was also fast, in that it was the first flying boat to exceed 500mph (800km/h). Power came from two Metropolitan-Vickers Beryl MVBI turbojets, mounted in the fuselage, each of 3,250–3,850lb thrust, with a large air-intake nose, while four 20-mm cannon provided the armament. The SR.A/1 flew well, which included making an inverted fly-past at the 1948 Farnborough Air Show, but the project was delayed by the need to find alternative engines for production machines, and in the end it was cancelled, one of the reasons for this being that the Saunders-Roe's distinctive flying-boat hull was thought to hamper its speed as a fighter.

This was certainly not true of the Convair Sea Dart, a seaplane fighter that used twin retractable skis in place of a conventional flying-boat hull,

allowing it to retain a more aerodynamic fuselage. The first prototype, built by U.S. manufacturer Convair, took off from San Diego Bay in April 1953, powered by two Westinghouse turbojets with a combined thrust of 8,500lbs (3855kg).

A second plane, the YF2Y-1, used the far more powerful Westinghouse J46 turbojets of 6,000lb thrust, each

The Convair Sea Dart, its twin hydro-skis deployed.

216

with afterburners. Thus equipped, the second Sea Dart was the first seaplane to exceed Mach 1, which it accomplished in a shallow dive from 34,000ft (10360m). A busy test programme followed, focusing on take-offs and landings using the surface of the water. Having no hull, the Sea Dart floated deep in the water, its wings only an inch or so above the surface; but on moving forward, the skis lifted it into hydroplane mode, ready for the take-off. Three more Sea Darts were built as part of the programme, but as with so many other promising projects, it never made it into production.

The Martin P6M Sea Master, a 1950s strategic flying-boat bomber for the U.S. Navy that almost entered service; production aircraft had been built and navy crews were already undergoing operational conversion when the programme was cancelled on 21 August 1959.

The Soviet Union had evidently learned its lesson from 1941, for it also began to develop jet-powered seaplanes after the Second World War. The U.S.S.R. also had an extensive coastline and inland lakes from which to base such planes, though it concentrated on bombers, long-distance transports, and anti-submarine craft rather than fighters. One of these was the longest, heaviest seaplane ever built.

The technical term for its type was a Power-Augmented Ram Wing in Ground Effect Machine (PAR-WIG), known to the Soviets more conveniently as an Ekranoplan, using the aerodynamic phenomenon of surface-effect. If an aircraft flies at a very low

The fourth Soviet KM Caspian Sea Monster Ekranoplan.

The YC-15 was McDonnell Douglas's entrant into the U.S.A.F.'s Advanced Medium STOL Transport competition, to replace the C-130 Hercules as the standard STOL tactical transport. In the end it was not ordered into production, although the YC-15's basic design would be used to form the successful C-17 Globemaster III.

altitude, equal to about half its wingspan, a cushion of air is built up between the wings and the surface (water, in this case), which reduces downwash and drastically cuts induced drag. This, of course, would be extremely hazardous over land, but is easily attainable over a calm sea. The

reduced drag in turn allows for higher speed and longer range, although the PAR-WIG planes also had the ability to fly normally.

The biggest of these was the aptly-named (by U.S. intelligence services) Caspian Sea Monster, eight of which were built from 1965, having a 131-ft

(40-m) wingspan and a massive overall length of 348ft (106m). Gross weight was up to 540 tonnes (it could carry 100 tonnes of cargo), and it had a range of 1,865 miles (3000km) and a cruising speed of 310mph (499km/h). Mostly based in the Caspian Sea, these giants failed to make it into modern times and the whole concept has since been largely forgotten. However, many countries besides the U.S.S.R. experimented with PAR-WIGS, including Germany with its small RFB X-114, powered by a single pusher propeller. At the other end of the scale, Boeing is studying the feasibility of a PAR-WIG that would dwarf even the Caspian Sea Monster. The Boeing

BELOW: The German RFB X-114 was powered by a Lycoming IO-360 four-cylinder aircraft engine driving a ducted propeller. It first flew in 1977.

OPPOSITE: The Ayers Loadmaster, designed for use by Federal Express.

WEIRD AIRCRAFT

ULTRA (Ultra Large Transport Aircraft) will, quite simply, be huge, with a 500-ft (152-m) wingspan and a capability of carrying 1,273 tonnes of cargo. Powered by four turboprop engines and skimming only 20–49ft (6–15m) above the water, Boeing predicts that it would have a range of 10,000 nautical miles. Now that really would be an incredible aircraft!

BIG RIGS OF THE SKY
Many children, growing up in the 1960s and '70s, found the

LEFT & BELOW: The Russian Beriev Be-200 is a multi-purpose amphibious aircraft, developed by the Beriev Aircraft Company as part of a co-operative project with Irkut. It is the largest fire-fighting plane in the world, and is designed to uplift a record volume of nearly 12 tonnes of water.

Thunderbirds puppet series fascinating. Every week, the Thunderbirds International Rescue team would perform heroic feats, using craft that could dive under water, fly

UPPERS & DOWNERS

The Fairchild XC-120 Pack-Plane.

supersonically, or carry prodigious loads. Thunderbird 2 was the cargo aircraft, able to carry huge pods, each one containing a different kind of specialized machinery, such as heavy-

duty cranes, earthmovers, or the 'Mole', which could burrow beneath wrecked buildings to save people trapped underground.

Of course, it was all science fiction, although of a particularly entertaining kind, but Thunderbird 2 really did exist,

in the form of the Fairchild XC-120 Pack-Plane. This was based on the twin-boom C119 Packet military transport, and first flew in August 1950. Instead of squeezing cargo into a conventional fuselage, and having to spend time loading/unloading before it could take

ABOVE & PAGES 226, 227 & 228: The Super Guppy is a large, wide-bodied U.S. cargo aircraft used for ferrying outsized cargo components. It was the successor to the Pregnant Guppy, the first of the Guppy aircraft produced by Aero Spacelines Inc. Five were built in two variants, both of which were colloquially referred to as Super Guppy.

off, the Pack-Plane's cargo fuselage was detachable. On landing, the plane could be unlocked from this mobile container, which could then be unloaded at leisure while the XC-120 took off with another. It had clamshell loading doors at both ends, able to swallow quite large military loads, which was an idea particularly attractive to military transport chiefs

who didn't want their planes spending excessive time on the tarmac, making them vulnerable to enemy action when they could be hauling tonnage through the skies. But despite performing well under test, the Pack-Plane failed to get further than the prototype stage.

It wasn't only the military that needed oversize transport aircraft, but

also the biggest user in modern times; the aerospace industry is perhaps best able to specify customized cargo carriers that might otherwise be sent by sea. One of the best-known of these was the Guppy, produced by Aero Spacelines in the early 1960s. NASA needed a quick and simple way of transporting huge but relatively light

components around the U.S.A. as part of the Apollo space programme, while at the same time, many U.S. airlines were retiring their Boeing 377 Stratocruisers. Former U.S.A.F. pilot John Conroy realized that an enlarged 377 had the potential to meet NASA's needs at a fraction of the cost of developing an all-new aircraft.

Aero Spacelines' Mini Guppy. Erickson Air Crane used this to haul heavy equipment until 1995, when it was retired to the Tillamook Air Museum in Oregon, where it resides to this day.

The Space Agency was lukewarm in its reaction to the idea, but Conroy was so convinced that it would work

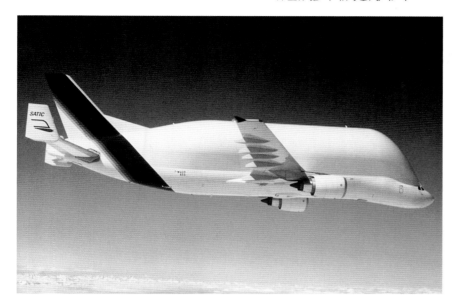

OPPOSITE, LEFT & BELOW: The *Airbus A300-600ST Beluga is a version of the standard A300-600 wide-body airliner, modified to carry aircraft parts and oversized or awkward cargo. At first, it was officially called the Super Transporter, but the name Beluga became popular and has now been officially adopted.*

that he mortgaged his house to build the prototype. Much of the airframe was unchanged, as were the four 3500-hp Pratt & Whitney R4360 radial piston engines, but a new 20-ft (6-m) diameter fuselage was added above the Stratocruiser's rear section, which was

detachable to allow Apollo rocket sections to be slid straight in.

Named the B-377B Pregnant Guppy (in a nod to NASA's original reaction to the idea), it first flew on 19 September 1962. NASA had evidently been won round, for the Guppy began carrying rocket parts for it the following summer. It proved a huge success, and Aero Spacelines bought another 25 aircraft to meet the demands of NASA's expanding programme. These included a Super Guppy, based on a Boeing C-97 cargo plane, which first flew in 1965, its bulbous fuselage hiding a gargantuan hold over 25-ft high and 25-ft (8-m) wide. The plane undertook much contract work for NASA, and proved so useful that the agency actually bought it out in 1979. Eventually, it was retired, and it is now preserved by the Pima Air and Space Museum in Tucson, Arizona.

Other guppies followed: the Mini Guppy's all-new fuselage made the hold wider than those of its predecessors. It first flew in 1969 and worked for various owners until retirement and preservation began to beckon. The Mini Guppy Turbine, powered by Allison 501 turboprops, had a shorter life, crashing in 1970 after only two months of flight-testing. But Aero Spacelines' final plane, the Super Guppy Turbine, which first flew that same year, was more successful, finding a new customer outside North America in the form of Airbus Industries in Europe. Two more were bought by the Europeans, who used the Super Guppy to haul wing and fuselage sections of Airbus planes from Britain and Germany to their final assembly plant at Toulouse, France.

These Guppies had been around for 25 years by the mid-1990s, and Airbus built its own replacement. Flying first in September 1994, the SATIC A300-600ST Super Transporter (also known as the Beluga) was based on the company's own A300-600 airliner, and like the Guppies, a bulbous cargo-carrying fuselage was added on top of the original, which allowed nearly 124ft (38m) of useable hold length and over 24ft (7m) of width. Its payload was over 45 tonnes. Powered by four GE CF6-80C2A8 engines, it could cruise at Mach 0.7 and climb to an altitude of 35,000ft (10670m). Not only did it ferry Airbus parts around Europe, but it is also one of the largest operating transport aircraft in the

world, the Beluga being in demand for carrying all sorts of unusual cargo, including a fuel tank for NASA's X-33 Venture Star spacecraft and *La Liberté guidant le peuple*, a valuable painting by Delacroix, which for its journey from France to Tokyo was sealed in an isothermally-protected pressurized tank – hardly the sort of cargo to be entrusted to baggage handlers and the hold of a routine 747!

OPPOSITE & BELOW: The Lockheed C-5 Galaxy is an American military transport aircraft, designed to provide strategic heavy airlift over intercontinental distances and to carry outsize and oversize cargo. The C-5 Galaxy has been operated by the U.S. Air Force since 1969 and is one of the largest military aircraft in the world.

CHAPTER SIX

PEOPLE'S PLANES

Many of the aircraft in this book are classed as remarkable because of their size and cost. But the reverse can also be true, and small and cheap can be just as incredible in their own way as large and expensive. The concept of a people's plane has been a constant theme running through aeronautical history. Rather like the dream of a people's car, that of an affordable, easy-to-fly machine, that would allow countless thousands to take to the skies independently, is certainly an alluring one. Of course, such dreams never take into account the traffic-control nightmare that would result, but that's another story. Ultimately, the concept of a people's plane is doomed to failure, however, because flying will never be as easy nor as cheap as running a small car, even though plenty of designers and

entrepreneurs have been more than eager to realize it.

By the 1920s, Henry Ford had already succeeded in building a people's car, as well as a people's tractor, so why not a cheap, mass-produced plane as well? In 1926 Ford displayed a prototype single-seater he referred to as the 'sky flivver'. It also flew, but when the Ford plane crashed two years later

on a test flight, killing the pilot, the whole project was abandoned.

The Frenchman Henri Mignet, however, had more lasting success. A furniture manufacture, he had failed to become a military pilot although his passion for flying had never diminished. He decided to build his own plane, testing the first prototypes from a large field north-east of Paris.

RIGHT & BELOW: The Loening M-2 Kitten of 1918 was used by the U.S. Navy, being ultra-light to enable it to operate from battleships or submarines.

The first successful Mignet was the HM-14, which flew in September 1933, and Henri Mignet would simply have been yet another DIY flying enthusiast had he been content with that; but he publicly demonstrated the HM-14 the following year and, in what was a revolutionary step, published the plans and building instructions for it,

Rul de Béziers constructed a tiny monoplane which was driven by a 5-hp motorcycle engine, allowing it to make several successful flights. The weight of the assembled plane was approximately 316lbs (143kg).

so that, in theory, anyone could build a Mignet replica, at minimal cost, for themselves. He named it the *Pou du Ciel*, literally, the Sky Louse, or perhaps rather more appealingly, the Flying Flea.

The Flying Flea was above all else extremely amenable, as far as reducing costs was concerned, being a single-seater staggered biplane built of wood and fabric. The HM-8 prototype had a wingspan of 19.5ft (6m), was 11.5-ft

(3.5-m) long, and was powered by a 17-hp 500-cc Aubier-Dunne motorcycle engine, giving it a useable speed range of 25–62mph (46–100km/h). It utilized a single control stick, the fore and aft movement of which controlled the front wing's angle of attack, increasing or decreasing lift, while side-to-side movement controlled the large rudder.

The Flying Flea was a two-axis aircraft, allowing it to take off or land only into the wind, so that pilots needed access to a large field. Mignet claimed that anyone with the ability to build a packing case and drive a car would be able to manage his aircraft.

In practice, unfortunately, this was not the case, and many Fleas crashed

BELOW: The De Havilland Tech School TK4, a single-seater monoplane racer that first flew in July 1937.

OPPOSITE: The Stits SA. 2 Sky Baby, claimed to be the world's smallest plane.

when their pilots were unable to recover from shallow dives. The problem had not arisen during prototype testing and only came to light when some began fitting more powerful engines than Mignet had envisaged. This was down to aerodynamic interference between the wings, and pulling the stick back (the pilot's natural reaction to a dive) only made the problem worse. The Royal Aircraft Establishment in Britain, and the French Air Ministry, conducted wind-tunnel tests and came up with a different airfoil and wing spacings that cured the problem; the later Fleas adopted this change.

The Flying Flea never could escape its reputation for being dangerous, but it remained popular with many enthusiasts. As soon as the plans were available, amateur builders got to work in the U.S.A. and France, and at least 500 were built in France alone. In one way, Henri Mignet's dream really had been fulfilled, for a Flying Flea could be built for about $350, which was for about the same price as a small car.

Many variants of the Flea followed, and Mignet Aviation continued building planes as well as

OPPOSITE: General Aircraft Limited's GAL 47 was designed to be an airborne air observation post (AOP) and had a twin-boom configuration and a pusher airscrew. Only one was built in 1940 at Hanworth Aerodrome, England.

BELOW: The first Wankel rotary-engined aircraft was the experimental Lockheed Q-Star civilian version of the U.S. Army's reconnaissance QT-2, basically a powered Schweizer sailplane, produced in 1968.

offering plans. But by 2008 it had ceased production of the HM-1100 Cordouan. In the Mignet tradition, this had been a tiny aircraft, though not quite as minimalist as the original Flying Flea. Powered by an 80-hp Jabiru 2200 engine, with a Rotax alternative, it had a claimed cruising speed of 99mph (159km/h), with a range of 270 miles (435km). Mignet Aviation also claimed that the plane was impossible to spin, also pointing out

that its fold-up wings made it easy to transport by road. Even if the company is no more, the hundreds of Flying Flea enthusiasts across the world have helped keep Henri Mignet's dream alive.

BUBBLE CRAFT

Strictly speaking, the Optica was never intended as a people's plane, though low cost had always been a part of the equation, making it an affordable alternative to the equivalent small

helicopter. It was designed in Britain by John Edgely, and first flew in December 1979, being a distinctive aircraft whose fully-glazed cabin could seat three abreast; this bulbous appendage made the Optica look more like an insect

than an aircraft, but it also afforded superb visibility. The Optica was intended for observation work, as the name suggests.

Behind the cabin was a Lycoming flat-six engine of 260-hp, powering a

ABOVE & OPPOSITE: The Edgely EA-7 Optica was a British light aircraft designed for observation work and intended to be a low-cost alternative to the helicopter.

pusher-ducted fan. There was a twin-boom cantilever tailplane with twin rudders and a high-mounted single elevator. The wings were simple, being unswept and untapered, and the whole plane was of conventional all-metal construction with a stressed aluminium skin. The Optica weighed less than a tonne and could reach 132mph (212km/h) with a 'loiter' cruise of 81mph (130km/h).

The Optica's announcement as a low-cost alternative to a light helicopter caused immense interest around the world. At $200,000 it was not expensive and promised low running costs; moreover, the fine visibility made it suitable for all sorts of tasks, including police work. In 1988, the UK police force tested the Optica's ground-search abilities against a Bolkow helicopter and an Islander light plane, while uniformed officers made a foot search on the ground.

WEIRD AIRCRAFT

OPPOSITE: The Fanliner 01 from Rheinflugzeugbau GmbH, a 1976 two-seater aircraft designed for sport and travel, powered by an RFB-modified Audi/NSU rotary engine driving an integrated ducted fan. The aircraft had a generous cabin layout offering a good field of vision and accessibility. The cabin was designed by Luigi Colani, a well-known stylist.

Their task was to find six 'bodies' in 1.25sq miles (3.2km^2) of heathland. Not only did the Optica find all six in 23 minutes, but it was worked out as the cheapest means of doing so, costing only £29 compared with the Islander's £95 and the helicopter's £106, while the officers on foot incurred a cost of over £4,000!

BELOW: The Rutan VariEze, a composite canard aircraft designed by Burt Rutan. It is a fairly high-performance home-build, hundreds of which have been constructed. The VariEze is notable for popularizing the canard configuration and mouldless composite construction for home-built aircraft. The first prototype flew on 21 May 1975.

The Gyroflug Speed Canard, an unconventional sports plane produced in Germany in the 1980s. Inspired by the Rutan VariEze, the Speed Canard was an all-new design created without input from Burt Rutan.

The Edgely Optica went into production in mid-1983, having been built by Brooklands Aircraft, and orders flooded in from all over the world. Sadly, it proved to be underdeveloped, and its fate was effectively sealed when an Optica, owned by the Hampshire Constabulary, crashed in May 1985, killing its two crew members. Sales collapsed and Edgely was made bankrupt. Production was revived twice in the 1980s, but finally ceased for good in March 1990.

The Eurowing EW-21 Goldwing.
This unusual single-seater aircraft was
constructed largely from glass fibre and
was thus very light in weight. It followed
similar design criteria as the VariEze and
Gyroflug Speed Canard.

FLYING CARS

There was another answer to the conundrum of a people's plane: the flying car. The reasoning behind it was impeccable, in that people likely to be in the market for an affordable aircraft would already be car-owners, so why not build a machine that could do both jobs – travel the skies as well as the roads. The concept of a flying car became a recurring theme of science fiction writers and illustrators, and we would all be driving/piloting to work in the early 21st century if some of those forecasters of the 1950s had been right.

Glenn Curtiss, a rival of the Wright brothers, actually designed a flying car, but it wasn't until March 1937 that such a beast actually took to the air. It was named the Aerobile, and was designed by Waldo Waterman, being a development of his tailless aircraft, the Whatsit. Powered by a Studebaker engine, the Aerobile could fly at 112mph (180km/h) but was limited to half that speed on the road.

It wasn't until after the Second World War that the subject of a flying car was again raised. Once again, Ford looked seriously at its potential, conducted a feasibility study, and

concluded that it was not only technically possible but could also be built at a realistic price. It was thought that the emergency services would be potential markets, as well as well-heeled private customers. However, the U.S. Federal Aviation Administration was less than impressed when Ford asked for its views, pointing to the difficulty of controlling massive amounts of private air traffic and policing drunken or irresponsible driver-pilots.

None of this deterred Moulton Taylor, however. Based in Longview, Washington, he designed the Aerocar which, though never reaching production, was the most successful of its kind ever conceived. He had been inspired to design the machine after meeting the inventor, Robert E. Fulton Jr., whose own Airphibian used detachable wings. Taylor realized that folding wings were a better solution, and used them in his flying car, which allowed it to be converted into flight

The Whatsit was a swept-wing, tailless aircraft, designed by Waldo Waterman between 1911 and 1932 when the prototype was finally in its testing phase. It was intended that it should be landed on the street and owned by regular people. It was later renamed the Waterman Arrowplane.

mode in just five minutes by one person. On the road, the wings and tail unit were towed by a car before being clipped on at the airfield, while flipping up the rear number plate allowed the owner to connect the propeller shaft and attach a pusher propeller.

The prototype was a success, capable of 60mph (100km/h) on the road and 110mph in the air, and gained

its civil certification in 1956. It was powered by a 135-hp Lycoming engine, had a range of 300 miles (483km) and a ceiling of 12,000ft (3658m), which for a light plane was a respectable performance. The car part of the Aerocar appeared exceptionally modest when compared with the chrome-laden American sedans fashionable at the time, and could carry only two people,

ABOVE, LEFT & PAGE 250: The Aerocar. Moulton B. Taylor was an aeronautical engineer famed for his work on developing a practical flying car. He trained as a U.S. Navy pilot, but spent much of the Second World War working on the navy's missile programme. Shortly after the war he designed his first flying car, the Aerocar, and founded a business, Aerocar International, to market it. To date, it remains the closest any such design came to actual mass-production, even though only six were ever built.

but it did the job. By American standards the Aerocar was tiny, weighing only 1,300lb (590kg) when empty, but in flying mode it was over 21-ft (6-m) long.

Once certification had been gained, Moulton Taylor reached an agreement with Ling-Temco-Vought to produce the Aerocar once 500 orders for it had

been received. Alas, only half that number of customers actually signed up for the deal and the production plans were dropped, even though six Aerocar prototypes had been built. One of these was still flying in 2006.

Since Moulton Taylor relinquished his dream, other prototype flying cars have come and gone, though none came

quite as close to becoming a production reality. Henry Smolinski's Mizar, however, was such a one. Developed in the early 1970s, it was the marriage of parts of a Cessna Skymaster with a Ford Pinto, and Smolinski claimed a cost for it starting from $18,000. According to some accounts, however, the prototype was seriously under-engineered, and it broke up during a test flight killing both Smolinski and the pilot.

More recently, the Moller M400, though not a true flying car, in that it cannot be driven on the road, claims to require no piloting knowledge at all, requiring only the desired direction and speed to be punched into its computer. Using eight Wankel rotary engines in place of conventional jets is claimed to save money, giving the Moller a maximium speed of 360mph

(580km/h), with a fuel consumption similar to that of a large car. But the M400 Skycar is still less than cheap, at around $1 million for the first production examples, moreover the production date has been continually postponed and the prototype has only ever made short-duration tethered flights.

But the world would be a duller place without such aircraft projects, however impractical they may be in the real world. In any case, most of the

The Moller M400 Skycar, a prototype personal VTOL flying car with four ducted fans, invented by Paul Moller, who has been attempting to develop such vehicles for many years. It is currently under development.

incredible aircraft described in this book were built for truly practical reasons, making them fitting testaments to human ambition, inventiveness, technology and, above all, lateral thinking.

ACKNOWLEDGEMENTS

Austin J Brown. Pages: 4, 18, 71, 98, 199. Cody Images. Pages: 5, 6, 11, 12, 13, 15, 16, 24 above, 25, 27, 28, 29, 30-31, 32, 33, 34, 37, 38 above & below, 39, 40, 41, 43, 47, 50, 52, 53 below, 54, 55, 56, 57, 60, 61, 67, 72, 73, 81, 82, 89, 90 both, 91, 92, 93, 94, 96, 97, 113, 114, 115, 116, 118, 119, 121, 126, 127, 128, 129, 130, 131, 132, 133, 134, 136, 140, 141, 143, 144, 145, 147, 149, 150, 162, 163, 164, 165, 166, 168, 169 below, 170, 171, 172, 173, 174 both, 175, 176, 177, 182 above, 183, 184, 185, 188, 191, 192, 203 above, 204, 205, 206, 210, 213, 217, 219, 221, 222, 223, 226, 228, 234, 235, 236 both, 237, 238, 239, 240, 241, 242, 243, 244, 246, 247, 248, 249 both, 250. Flickr Creative Commons and the following:- Pages: 58 Moody 75, 59 Alan Light, 77 Georgio, 85, 85, 111 above, Armchair Aviator, 160 James Gordon. NASA. Pages: 74, 75, 142, 146, 148, 152, 156, 157, 158. Philip Jarrett Collection. Pages: 2, 8, 9, 17, 24 below, 45, 46, 78, 79, 80, 88 below, 110, 120, 122, 125. Regency House Publishing Ltd.

Pages: 10, 21, 22, 23, 62-63, 64, 69 below, 103 above, 104, 105, 106, 107, 108, 112, 124, 135, 153, 154 above, 178, 179, 180-181, 182 below, 187, 189, 193, 194, 198, 200, 210, 207, 208, 210, 212, 214, 216, 220, 224, 231 above, 251. Page 87: Shawn Aro. United States Airforce. Pages: 3, 20, 26, 66, 70, 99, 101, 138, 154, 155, 202, 203 below, 230, 232. United States Army. Page: 95.Via Russian Aviation Research Trust. Pages: 35, 48, 53 above, 65, 218. Wikimedia Creative Commons and the following:- Pages: 68 United States Airforce, 69 above, 103 below, 111 below United States Federal Government, 76, United States Airforce/Master Sgt. Dave Casey, 83 William S. Porter, 88 above Keith Edkins, 100 John McCullagh, 102 Ben-pcc, 151 Bezuk, 159, 186, 225, 227 NASA, 167 Hanna Reitsch, 169 above Fair Use Rationale, 190 Adam Hunt, 195 Wikimedia, 197 United States Airforce/Staff Sgt, Marcus Maier, 229 SpiralOut, 231 below Xeper, 233 United States Airforce/Brett Snow, 245 Arpingstone.